7 DAY *VEGAN* CHALLENGE

BETTINA CAMPOLUCCI BORDI

Hardie Grant

BOOKS

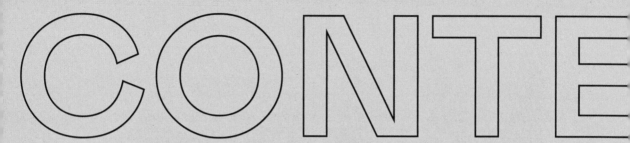

CONTE

NTS

A LITTLE ABOUT BETTINA'S KITCHEN

To really understand my background and where my love of food began, I'm going to go back to the very beginning. My father is Norwegian my mother Bulgarian-Danish. And me? Well, I was born in Denmark, but spent the first 11 years of my life in Tanzania, East Africa, before my family relocated to Sweden. In Tanzania, we were very connected with the food that was put on the table; I used to go with my mother to the markets to pick our fruits and vegetables for the week, and quickly learned the art of haggling for best quality and price. All of our dairy products would come from local small holdings, and on the journey home from the farm, I would sit in the back of the car with a bucket full of fresh milk that my mother would then magically turn into butter, cream and yoghurt. So in all this, I learnt early on that good things were worth waiting for – in fact, there is a running family joke about my father taking his time to cook, because by the time the food is ready we are all starving, such is his meticulousness in preparing every element of a dish.

Most of our holidays were spent in Bulgaria with my grandmother and auntie, who were both amazing cooks; I used to sit at the kitchen table at my auntie's house watching her make pineapple upside-down cake, creme brûlée, stews and breads baked from scratch. The rest of our summers were spent in Sweden with my other grandmother. Again, she was an amazing cook with green fingers, too, and had all sorts of wonders growing in her garden and a tiny summer house in the woods. Jams, cordials and pickling were her speciality. All this is to say that I come from the sort of family that does not remember visits to museums or art galleries – my holidays were filled with food experiences. We travelled extensively as a family, gathering food memories and that have stayed on with me to this day. I love travelling, sampling and experiencing cultures and countries through food. There are so many untold stories everywhere, and they often play a huge part of our lives – that's how I initially caught the cooking bug that has blossomed into a life-encompassing passion.

I began working in the wellness industry over seven years ago when I started running health retreats in Spain. Following some struggles with personal health issues, including Polycystic Ovary Syndrome (PCOS) and Endometriosis, I soon discovered that what I ate made a significant impact on my physical health, to the point that it helped me manage my conditions and made a profoundly positive effect on my mental wellbeing, too. Despite doctors' prognosis, I was able to fall pregnant and bring my beautiful daughter into the world in the following years. Cooking became a way of inspiring people to include and cook with ingredients that can sometimes be daunting. I wanted to show others how cooking from scratch is the single most powerful thing you can do for yourself and your family.

Cooking at retreats started as a hobby, but it quickly transformed into a career as a chef in plant-based cuisine. From that point, I began to specialise in gluten-free and free-from cooking, which form the foundations of recipes and workshops to this day. I went on to study courses at the Matthew Kenney Culinary Academy in Los Angeles to expand my cooking skills and knowledge, and travelled extensively to discover how other cultures use plant foods. I started sharing recipes on Instagram, and slowly but surely it gathered pace: Bettina's Kitchen was born, and today encompasses culinary, yoga and mindfulness retreats, plant-based cooking workshops, recipe development, food writing, and most recently, my cookbooks: the first, *Happy Food*, the second being the book you are holding in your hands.

Everything I do honours my own beliefs around food and wellness and aligns with my philosophies: that we should eat seasonally, locally and from farm-to-table as much as we can, support small businesses within our communities, and use roots, shoots and all. Cooking waste free is particularly important to me, and I truly believe that we must let our veggies do the talking – the best plant food is fuss-free, simple, easy, inexpensive and speaks for itself.

My knowledge of and passion for plant-based foods continues to grow and I am constantly on the hunt for delicious solutions to the belief that eating plants is boring, expensive and time consuming. I hope that I can help to inspire you to incorporate more plants into your diet, provide a starting point for your journey and show you just how easy cooking with plants can be. I believe we can start now to positively influence the next generation in the importance of true self-care and choices so that, unlike us, they don't have to relearn them later in life. This includes sourcing local ingredients in any shape or form, preserving traditions, eating seasonally and cooking from scratch.

VEGANISM:
WHAT'S ALL THE FUSS ABOUT?

The term 'vegan' is said to have been coined in the 1940s by Donald Watson, the founder of the Vegan Society, as a way of describing non-dairy vegetarians. *Collins English Dictionary* defines a vegan as 'a person who refrains from using any animal product whatever for food, clothing or any other purpose'.

Most of the labels – like pescatarian, freegan and lacto-ovo vegetarian – are created to identify one's way of eating. Vegan, on the other hand, is not something related to food only, but to a whole way of living aimed at reducing any sort of animal exploitation with regard to your lifestyle and the materials you use on a daily basis.

So is this a pro-vegan book?

The short answer is 'no, this is not a vegan lifestyle book'. It's an inclusive book that embraces everyone from the full-on vegans to those who know it makes good sense to eat more veg. It's a pro-plant book that simply gives you the tools to try vegan food for 7, 10, 21 or any number of days that you wish.

If you decide to go vegan after giving it a go, that's entirely up to you. I make no judgement! I am a firm believer in helping you find out what suits you and giving you the freedom to go with what makes you feel good. If anything, I just hope this book gives you the inspiration to add as many plants as possible to your diet in an easy and delicious way.

WHAT IS THE CHALLENGE, & WHY SHOULD I DO IT?

Have you heard a lot about the benefits of going vegan? And about the downsides? Are you interested in giving it a try? Or perhaps you've made your decision but aren't quite sure how to go about it.

The challenge is to go vegan for seven days – simple! This book will help you by offering up three different menu plans to choose from: The Easy Peasy Way (see page 148) is for the go-getters – the ones who do not mind having the same meals over and over again as long as it fits in with their lifestyle, and its filling and nutritious. Then there is the weekly menu for The Planners (see page 150) – this is for people who like to be organised, and don't mind batch cooking and preparing beforehand if it means being able to throw together meals quickly during the week. Last but not least, there is the Fast and Fresh plan (see page 152), which covers recipes that are quick to cook from scratch when needed, but might require putting a bit more effort in than just making a sandwich – although don't get me wrong, this book has those too. Regardless what plan you choose, *7 Day Vegan Challenge* is filled with easy recipes, accessible ingredients, short methods and most importantly, plenty of options.

Whatever your motivation, the *7 Day Vegan Challenge* is designed to help you give it a go. It is a super-easy and convenient way for anyone to test-drive a vegan diet, including a whole new array of ingredients and combinations on your plate, so you can see how varied, healthy and imaginative it can be. There are so many different grain and seed options that are available for you to discover. And a whole new world of flours about to open up for you. In all the recipes, I have made a conscious effort to increase the plant versus grain proportions, and the recipes also offer you serving options so you can adapt the dishes from simple, after-work suppers to something a bit more fancy for entertaining at the weekend when you have a little more time and inclination. This challenge also happens to be gluten free – not because there is anything wrong with gluten, but because it is what I happen to specialise in.

WHAT ARE BOOSTERS?

One unique feature of this book is the 'boosters' that you will find in almost all the recipes. View them as little powerhouses of nutrition designed to splash or sprinkle on your finished dish to amp up the nutritional value of your meals. They contain things like good fats, vitamins, minerals and antioxidants – oh, and they add an extra level of flavour, too. So you'll find chillies, hemp hearts and all kinds of nuts and seeds to boost your healthy eating. They should all be available in major supermarkets or health food stores.

A LITTLE NOTE ON EQUIPMENT

You don't need any special equipment for the simple and recognisable cooking methods in this book. I do use a blender a lot, so that's the only essential, but even a handheld blender with the attachment will do fine.

And in order to do my bit for the environment, I prefer to use glass containers and bottles for buying and storing food instead of plastic.

WASTE NOT

I chose to create recipes that cater for two persons from the start and which can easily be multiplied, rather than the more usual four servings in most books. This is because there are many smaller households not catered for in terms of cookbooks, and many of us tend to cook too much and be left with leftovers that don't get eaten.

I have made a conscious decision to use the same ingredients in many of the recipes, so that you will not need a pantry filled with fancy ingredients to be able to cook from this book. Also you will minimise waste as one kilo of carrots, for example, will lend itself well to several of the recipes.

Another time-saving and waste-saving option is the traybake section, where you can have one to two portions but leave the rest for later and have an extra portion handy to bring to work.

I made sure that the recipes are simple and easy to follow, so that you don't spend too much time planning or preparing for your meals.

A NOTE ON INGREDIENTS

I am a firm believer in following the seasons; produce tastes better, is often better priced and you get to support local farms and businesses. If you don't have the time to go to farmers' markets, then subscribing to a local veggie box can be a great option. Trial your way through a few until you find the perfect fit. You might not get it all right immediately – finding good produce or a service that fits your lifestyle can take time and effort – but, trust me, it'll be worth it in the end.

WHAT HAPPENS WHEN THE CHALLENGE IS OVER?

Thats up to you! You can continue for as many days as you like or choose to implement some of what you have learnt along the way a few days a week. There is no pressure here. The challenge has been designed to be a fun way of including and introducing new ways of eating more plants. Hopefully this book will make that happen! My biggest advice would be to make sure that you eat enough. This is not a diet book. Have fun in the process and best of luck! I'll be rooting for you and supporting you along the way.

FREQUENTLY ASKED
QUESTIONS ABOUT VEGANISM

IS VEGANISM HEALTHY?

Here's the short answer: it depends on what you eat, whether you cook from scratch, and whether you eat vegetables and a varied diet (some vegans don't like vegetables and get stuck eating pasta, bread and rice, as do meat-eaters).

Here's the long answer: no diet, neither meat-based nor plant-based, is healthy and complete nutritionally speaking 'just because'. Any dietary choice can be healthy or unhealthy. What you are looking for is a balanced diet that contains all the nutritional elements in the correct proportions. So while it would be technically vegan to live on potato chips, cookies, squidgy bread and soda, that certainly wouldn't constitute a healthy or balanced diet.

The truth is that the Western diet is a cause for huge concern. Many people aren't thriving. The rising rates of diabetes, high blood pressure, heart disease, some types of cancer, auto-immune disease and other chronic, diet-related illnesses are astonishing and prove that we are not eating in a balanced way. Of course, these illnesses are complex and brought on by multiple causes, some that have nothing to do with diet, but there is an extensive body of research telling us that there are direct links between diet and disease. We see this on a daily basis in studies and the media.

If you decide to go fully vegan and make the switch as a family, it would be a good idea to consult a qualified nutritionist to make sure you are covering the basics in your transition, especially if it's a forever decision and children are involved.

SHOULD YOU COOK FROM SCRATCH?

Cooking from scratch makes a huge difference to how you eat. Plenty of the recipes in this book have really short ingredients lists, making it easy for you to source your ingredients responsibly and putting you in control of what goes into your pot.

What's more, the recipes are simple to prepare and cook; while the act of cooking is an act of self-care itself! So I recommend you cook from scratch and include more of the plant kingdom in your life now that you have this wonderful book as a base, and trial and error the recipes that you like and then you can include them in your weekly repertoire!

WHERE DO YOU GET YOUR PROTEIN?

This is something you will be asked on many occasions. First let's break protein down a little bit. Protein is a macronutrient that is made up of chains of aminoacids, and we get these from the food we eat, either plant or animal. Our bodies are capable of combining the amino acids we eat and using them like building blocks to create protein. The body does not differentiate whether these amino acids came from a cow or a bean, provided we get enough of them.

You don't need to obsess over counting the grams you take in, just make sure you're eating plenty of protein-rich foods throughout the day and your body will look after the rest!

IS VEGAN FOOD MORE EXPENSIVE?

As with everything, there are lots of brands and foods that latch on to the hottest-selling trend. You will see many foods at the supermarket suddenly labelled 'vegan' because an increasing number of people are interested. But, as we've seen, the label 'vegan' does not necessarily mean healthy. You don't need to spend loads of money on fancy tinctures, super powders and expensive ingredients. I recommend that you start with the basics – good-quality veggies, fruits, nuts, seeds, pulses and grains – and take it from there.

WHY SHOULD I GIVE IT A GO?

Everyone, no matter what diet they follow, should pay attention to what goes on their plates. To me, once you learn the basics, eating vegan isn't just sufficient, it can also be incredibly healthy, and it's actually quite simple. And this book is filled with nutritious and delicious recipes to suit your trial. What's more, we've done all the planning for you in the weekly menus (see page 146), so all you have to do is go and get your supplies and get cooking!

So try it for a week and see how you feel. Then you can make up your mind whether or not you want to stick with the vegan option and how you would like to apply it to your life, whether it's a forever thing or just a few meals a week. It's all about adding those veggies.

COOK'S NOTES

○ Use medium-sized fruit and vegetables.

○ Use fresh ingredients, including herbs and spices.

○ Do not mix metric, imperial and US measures.

○ 1 teaspoon = 5 ml; 1 tablespoon = 15 ml.

○ Only peel vegetables if necessary. For example, I only peel ginger if it is not organic.

○ All ovens vary in their cooking temperatures, so you need to get to know yours. Check with the manufacturer's instructions and, if necessary, use an oven thermometer. The temperatures given in this book are the conventional style, but these should be treated as a guide only. If you are cooking in a new fan-assisted oven, you should decrease the temperatures by 10–20°C (50–68°F).

○ Items in cups should be loosely packed.

○ You can use any plant milk – unsweetened almond, coconut or, my favourite, oat milk.

○ Where you see a freezer symbol, an element of the dish will be suitable to freeze, but in general, fresh ingredients used to garnish, e.g. fruit, avocado, herbs or raw vegetables, should be added once reheated.

○ The icons at the top of each recipe indicate:

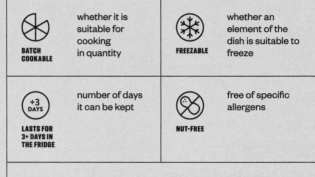

BATCH COOKABLE	whether it is suitable for cooking in quantity	FREEZABLE	whether an element of the dish is suitable to freeze
+3 DAYS LASTS FOR 3+ DAYS IN THE FRIDGE	number of days it can be kept	NUT-FREE	free of specific allergens

BOOSTER

These are ingredients you can sprinkle on the top of your finished dish to add extra nutritional value

BREKK
ON TH
& ONT
SLOW

Breakfast is my favourite meal of the day. We have
a special rule in our house that I think is worth sharing:
*no screen time until work or after the school run
and you've arrived at work.* That means phones are
switched off once the alarm has gone and mornings
are spent getting ready and eating breakfast together
(if there is time). We love our digital-free mornings. I
always make sure I have something nourishing and
filling even if it is on the go.

SMOOTHIE ON THE GO

I find many smoothies fill me up fast but then I feel hungry again equally quickly, so this is my go-to, slow-release concoction that will keep you feeling full for longer. I love oat milk, but you can use any plant milk.

Put all the ingredients into a blender and blitz until you have a smooth beauty on your hands. Drink straight away or take it along with you to work.

MAKES 1 PORTION

500 ml (17 fl oz/2 cups) Oat Milk
(see page 142) or other plant milk
1 handful of frozen blueberries
1 medjool date, pitted
1 tablespoon oat bran
1 teaspoon hemp hearts
1 tablespoon peanut butter

BOOSTER

1 teaspoon flaxseed oil

THREE-WAY PORRIDGE

Porridge is one of my go-to breakfasts – quick, easy and 100 per cent satisfying. To switch things up a bit and maximise plant intake, I have increased the ratio of fruit to oats and also given you grain options so that you can experiment to discover which you like best. These can be made and left overnight to serve cold in the morning if you prefer.

BATCH COOKABLE

FREEZABLE

NUT-FREE

MOSTLY APPLES & OAT PORRIDGE

Grate the apples, including the core and peel, and set aside.

Gently heat up the coconut oil in a small pan, then add the spices and gently give them a stir. Add the oats and plant milk and bring to a simmer for 5 minutes until thickened and the oats are soft, stirring occasionally. Take the pan off the heat and ladle in the grated apple.

Enjoy with milk and a dollop of nut butter, jam or plant yoghurt.

MAKES 2 PORTIONS

2 eating (dessert) apples
½ teaspoon coconut oil
½ teaspoon ground cinnamon
½ teaspoon ground cardamom
1 pinch of ground cloves
125 g (4 oz/1 cup) oats (or quinoa, rice, millet or buckwheat flakes)
500 ml (17 fl oz/2 cups) Oat Milk (see page 142) or other plant milk
plant milk, nut butter, jam or plant yoghurt, to serve

BOOSTERS

hemp hearts
chopped nuts

BANOFFEE OATS

BATCH COOKABLE

FREEZABLE

NUT-FREE

Peel and mash the bananas and set aside. Gently heat up the coconut oil in small pan, add the vanilla paste, then gently stir in the dates. Add the oats, plant milk and salt and bring to a simmer for 5 minutes until thickened and the oats are soft, stirring occasionally. Take the pan off the heat and ladle in the mashed bananas.

Enjoy with a dollop of coconut yoghurt.

MAKES 2 PORTIONS

2 bananas
½ teaspoon coconut oil
1 teaspoon vanilla paste
2 medjool dates, pitted and torn
125 g (4 oz/1 cup) oats (or quinoa, rice, millet, buckwheat flakes)
500 ml (17 fl oz/2 cups) Oat Milk (see page 142) or other plant milk
a pinch of salt
coconut yoghurt, to serve

BOOSTERS

grated dark dairy-free chocolate (with at least 70% cocoa solids)
cacao nibs
hemp hearts
chopped nuts

BATCH COOKABLE

FREEZABLE

NUT-FREE

SPICY CARROT OATS

Gently heat the coconut oil in small saucepan, then add the cinnamon and stir gently. Add the oats and plant milk and bring to a simmer for 5 minutes until thickened and the oats are soft, stirring occasionally. Take the pan off the heat and ladle in the carrots and the currants.

Enjoy with a dollop of nut butter or a handful of chopped nuts, if using.

MAKES 2 PORTIONS

½ teaspoon coconut oil
½ teaspoon ground cinnamon
125 g (4 oz/1 cup) oats (or quinoa, rice, millet, buckwheat flakes)
500 ml (17 fl oz/2 cups) Oat Milk (see page 142) or other plant milk
2 carrots, grated
1 tablespoon currants
nut butter or chopped nuts or seeds, to serve (optional)

BOOSTERS

hemp hearts
cacao nibs

BATCH COOKABLE

FREEZABLE

SWEET QUINOA

This is a ridiculously easy recipe. It's crunchy, filling, fresh and jam-packed with goodness – with no added sweeteners. It makes a great breakfast to take away, batch cook or even enjoy as a dessert.

Precook the quinoa according to the packet instructions or use a packet of ready-made quinoa. Chop the apple, pear and orange into small squares (smaller than bite size) and put in a bowl. Add all the remaining ingredients and give it a really good stir.

Enjoy with an added dollop of plant yoghurt, a few mint leaves or a sprinkling of seasonal fruits.

MAKES 2 PORTIONS

130 g (4½ oz/1 cup) precooked
   quinoa (any colour)
1 eating (dessert) apple
1 pear
1 orange, peeled
juice of ½ blood orange or orange
juice of ½ lemon
1 tablespoon raisins
1 tablespoon chopped almonds
1 teaspoon ground cinnamon
1 teaspoon ground cardamom
1 pinch of ground cloves
plant yoghurt, mint leaves
   or seasonal fruits, to serve

BOOSTERS

sesame seeds
chopped nuts

BATCH COOKABLE

FREEZABLE

NUT-FREE

POLENTA WITH WARM BERRIES

In this porridge culture of ours, it's nice to try something new. Polenta has such a lovely creamy texture and, paired with warm berries, it's a match made in heaven.

Put the polenta and plant milk in a medium-sized pan and gently bring to the boil. Turn the heat down to a simmer and cook for 5 minutes, stirring so that it doesn't catch on the bottom of the pan, until thick and creamy. When it is ready, stir in the plant cream and vanilla paste. Set aside.

Meanwhile, put the frozen berries in a separate small pan with the water and warm through over a low heat for 5 minutes.

Spoon some of the creamy polenta into bowls, stir in the apple syrup, if using, and top with a spoonful of warm berries. This is best eaten straight away.

MAKES 2 PORTIONS

100 g (3½ oz/⅔ cup) polenta
500 ml (17 fl oz/2 cups) Oat Milk
   (see page 142) or other plant milk
60 ml (2 fl oz/¼ cup) Plant Cream
   (cashew, almond or sunflower)
   (see page 142)
1 teaspoon vanilla paste
125 g (4 oz/scant ⅔ cup) mixed
   frozen berries
splash of water
dash of apple syrup (optional)

BATCH COOKABLE

FREEZABLE

LASTS FOR 2+ DAYS IN THE FRIDGE

NUT-FREE

BREAKFAST BURRITOS

I love this recipe. I always make a large batch of the mince and keep it readily available in the fridge or freezer so that I can put together a meal in minutes. It's versatile and absolutely delicious.

Heat the oil in a saucepan, add the leek and garlic and fry for about 5 minutes over a low heat until nice and soft, stirring occasionally. Season with cayenne and salt and pepper to taste. Then add the drained beans and fry for another 5 minutes over a medium heat, stirring occasionally. Give them a good stir, then separate half of the mixture in the pan and gently mash with the back of a fork. You will end up having a mince-like texture with some lovely crispy bits in there. Take the mixture off the heat and add the raw red onion and pineapple and give it a mix.

Assemble the burritos by spooning some avocado on your tortillas and mashing it in with the back end of your fork. Add the mince, tomato, lettuce and coriander.

This is lovely with a dollop of plant yoghurt and a squeeze of lime juice or a spoonful of chilli jam. It perfectly hits that savoury spot!

MAKES 2 PORTIONS

2 tablespoons olive oil
½ leek, green and all, chopped
1–2 garlic cloves, chopped
½ teaspoon cayenne
250 g (9 oz/1 cup) tinned black beans, well drained
¼ red onion, finely chopped
20 g (¾ oz) chopped fresh or tinned pineapple
salt and freshly cracked black pepper

FOR THE BURRITO ASSEMBLY

2 corn or wheat tortillas
½ avocado, peeled, pitted and chopped
1 tomato, chopped
2 lettuce leaves, shredded
a few coriander (cilantro) leaves
plant yoghurt, lime juice or chilli jam, to serve

BOOSTER

hemp hearts

BATCH COOKABLE

FREEZABLE

FLUFFY ONE-PAN APPLE PANCAKE

I make this every week and everyone loves it. It makes a great batch cook, and the batter keeps fresh in the fridge for several days so you can make pancakes on demand. It uses what I call a flax 'egg': 1 tablespoon flaxseed meal and 2 tablespoons water. You can buy flaxseed meal or blitz flaxseeds in a blender.

In a large mixing bowl, whisk together the flaxseed meal and water and let it set for 1–2 minutes. Add the peanut butter, baking powder, bicarbonate of soda, salt and vanilla paste and whisk everything together well. Add the plant milk and whisk again until well combined.

Next add the oat and buckwheat flours, stir until combined, then let the batter rest for 5 minutes. Alternatively, the batter can be prepped for the next day; sometimes the pancakes become even tastier if they have rested in the fridge.

To cook the pancakes, preheat a small frying pan (skillet) so it is hot but not so screaming hot that the oil smokes when it makes contact with the surface of the pan. Add a little coconut oil to the pan, then gently lay the apple slices in the pan and fry for 5 minutes until lightly browned on each side. Arrange the apples beautifully in the pan.

Give the batter a stir, then pour in the pancake batter and cook for about 5 minutes until the surface bubbles, then flip the pancake over with a large slice and fry on the other side until cooked through. Serve with a dollop of jam or plant yoghurt.

MAKES 1 LARGE PANCAKE, ENOUGH FOR 2 PORTIONS

1 tablespoon flaxseed meal
2 tablespoons water
2 tablespoons peanut butter
1 teaspoon baking powder
1 pinch of bicarbonate of soda (baking soda)
1 pinch of salt
1 teaspoon vanilla paste
250 ml (8½ fl oz/1 cup) Oat Milk (see page 142) or other plant milk
100 g (3½ oz/scant 1 cup) oat flour
100 g (3½ oz/1 cup) buckwheat flour
1 tablespoon coconut oil
1–2 large eating (dessert) apples, peeled, cored and sliced into wedges
jam or plant yoghurt, to serve

BOOSTERS

nut butter
chopped nuts
hemp hearts

SAVOURY GINGER & GARLIC OATS

This is my take on a savoury Moorish porridge bowl, married with the flavours of warming ginger and garlic. I know this might sound like a strange combination but, trust me, it does work.

Heat the olive oil in a saucepan and add the garlic, leek and ginger and fry for 5 minutes until soft. Crumble in the stock cube, then add the oats, followed by the water and bring to a simmer. Continue to simmer, stirring occasionally, for a good 5 minutes until thick and creamy.

Meanwhile, heat a small pan and add the kale and bok choy and a sprinkle of water and heat over a medium heat for a couple of minutes to soften the leaves. Add the tamari and stir through, then set aside.

Once the porridge has thickened, ladle a few spoonfuls into a bowl and top with the beautiful wilted greens and the finely chopped spring onion. Eat immediately while still warm.

MAKES 2 PORTIONS

1 teaspoon olive oil
1–2 garlic cloves, chopped
½ leek, green and all, chopped
1 thumb-sized piece of ginger, peeled and chopped
½ vegan stock cube
120 g (3½ oz/1 cup) oats
625 ml (21 fl oz/generous 2½ cups) water, plus a sprinkling for the green vegetables
1 handful of kale, chopped
1–2 pak choy (bok choy), chopped
1 tablespoon tamari
1 spring onion (scallion), green and all, finely chopped

BOOSTERS

splash of sesame oil
hemp hearts

**BATCH
COOKABLE**

FREEZABLE

+4
DAYS

**LASTS FOR
4+ DAYS IN
THE FRIDGE**

NUT-FREE

TENDER GREENS ON TOAST WITH PEA HUMMUS OR AJVAR ROASTED PEPPER SPREAD

I love good toasties – they should never be underestimated. So easy to put together, they are gloriously filling when you need that hit of savoury and spicy with a boost of greens. This recipe makes a large batch of hummus, which will store in the fridge for several days. It is also my husband's favourite breakfast and snack!

To make the hummus, put all the hummus ingredients into a blender and blitz until you have a nice smooth texture, adding a little more water along the way if needed to reach the texture and smoothness that you prefer. Store in a glass jar in the fridge and consume within 3 days.

To make the roasted pepper spread, first fry the aubergine for 5–10 minutes with a little olive oil, until soft. Put all the spread ingredients into a blender and pulse until you have a nice chunky consistency – you still want to see bits of parsley in your mixture. Store in a glass jar in the fridge and consume within 4–5 days.

To make the toasties, put a griddle pan over a medium heat, add the olive oil and heat, then turn up the heat to high, add the broccoli and kale and cook for a few minutes until charred. Season to taste with salt and pepper, then set aside. Meanwhile, toast the bread.

To assemble, rub the garlic on your toast and generously spread your chosen spread on top, then finish with the griddled greens and eat straight away while still hot. If you're a spicy kind of person, sprinkle over a few chilli flakes.

MAKES 2 PORTIONS

FOR THE PEA HUMMUS

240 g (8½ oz/1 cup) drained tinned
  chickpeas (garbanzos)
juice of 1 lemon
120 ml (4 fl oz/½ cup) light roast
  tahini (sesame paste)
1 garlic clove
100 g (3½ oz/⅔ cup) frozen peas
60 ml (2 fl oz/¼ cup) water

**FOR THE AJVAR ROASTED
PEPPER SPREAD**

½ aubergine (eggplant)
300 g (10½ oz) grilled jarred
  red peppers, drained
2 garlic cloves
2 tablespoons olive oil
30 g (1 oz) parsley

FOR THE TOASTIES

2 tablespoons olive oil
200 g (7 oz) tenderstem broccoli
1 handful of kale, chopped
2 slices of bread (sourdough
  or good-quality gluten-free)
1 garlic clove, halved
salt and freshly cracked black pepper
1 pinch of chilli (hot pepper) flakes

BOOSTERS

hemp hearts
sesame seeds

CHICKPEA SCRAMBLE

BATCH COOKABLE

FREEZABLE

+1 DAY

LASTS FOR 1+ DAYS IN THE FRIDGE

NUT-FREE

Such a brilliant, filling meal – with plenty of delicious veggies and made in no time! You can serve it for breakfast, lunch or dinner – whatever floats your boat.

Put a large saucepan over a medium heat and add the olive oil, leek and pepper and fry for about 5–10 minutes until soft and lightly browned. Put half the chickpeas into a blender and blitz, then add to the pan with the remaining unblended chickpeas, stir well and simmer for another few minutes until heated through. Sprinkle in the paprika and chilli and season with salt and pepper to taste. Finally add the spinach and let it wilt into the mixture.

This is great served with fresh cherry tomatoes, toast and slices of avocado.

MAKES 2 PORTIONS

2 tablespoons olive oil
1 small or ½ large leek, green and all, chopped
½ red (bell) pepper, finely diced
240 g (8½ oz/1 cup) drained tinned chickpeas (garbanzos)
1 tablespoon sweet paprika
1 pinch of chilli (hot pepper) flakes
salt and freshly cracked black pepper
100 g (3½ oz) spinach leaves
cherry tomatoes, toast and avocado slices, to serve

BOOSTER

hemp hearts

**BATCH
COOKABLE**

FREEZABLE

+7
DAYS

**LASTS FOR
+7 DAYS IN
THE FRIDGE**

NUT-FREE

AVOCADO BENEDICT

This is an awesome brunch or dinner option that looks pretty impressive, too, so makes either a tasty weekday meal or even something more special for the weekend. The mayonnaise will last a week in an airtight 250 ml (8½ fl oz) jar in the fridge and goes well with pretty much everything. Aquafaba is the liquid from a tin of chickpeas, so keep it in an airtight jar in the fridge when you have used chickpeas in another recipe; it will last 3–4 days in the fridge.

To make the mayonnaise, heat the olive oil in a small frying pan (skillet), add the shallot and fry over a medium heat for about 5 minutes until soft and lightly browned. Leave to cool. Alternatively, you can use shop-bought vegan mayo and add the seasoning and chopped herbs.

Put the aquafaba, lemon juice, mustard and apple cider vinegar in a bowl and whisk until combined. Keep whisking while you gradually add the rapeseed oil until the mixture emulsifies and starts coming together as a mayonnaise. Continue whisking and slowly add the olive oil until it has all been incorporated. Season to taste with salt and pepper. Stir in the shallots and the tarragon and mix well with a hand mixer or whisk.

Rinse the kale and put it in a saucepan with just the water clinging to the leaves. Put the pan over a low heat for a few minutes until the kale has wilted.

Toast the sourdough bread, then top with the kale and avocado slices, and a dollop of the tarragon mayonnaise and a sprinkling of dill fronds or chives for extra yumminess.

MAKES 2 PORTIONS

1 large handful of kale,
   roughly chopped
2 slices of sourdough bread
1 avocado, peeled, stoned
   and sliced
a few dill fronds or snipped chives

**FOR THE TARRAGON
& SHALLOT MAYO**

60 ml (2 fl oz/¼ cup) olive oil
1 shallot, chopped
3½ tablespoons aquafaba
   (liquid from tinned chickpeas/
   garbanzos)
1 tablespoon lemon juice
1 teaspoon Dijon mustard
1 teaspoon apple cider vinegar
120 ml (4 fl oz/½ cup) organic
   rapeseed oil (organic is usually
   a lot yellower)
1 pinch of salt and freshly cracked
   black pepper
20 g (¾ oz) tarragon leaves,
   chopped

BATCH COOKABLE

FREEZABLE

NUT-FREE

CHINESE OMELETTE

This is my savoury go-to breakfast. It reminds me of holidays in Asia amongst palm trees, beaches and humid curly hair. So good on any given day!

Heat the olive oil in a pan, add the garlic, Chinese leaves and carrot and fry for 5–10 minutes, until nice and soft. Add the tamari, sesame seeds and sesame oil and put the heat right down and leave.

Put all the omelette ingredients apart from the sesame seeds in a mixing bowl and whisk until smooth, then leave to stand for 5 minutes. Get a non-stick pan nice and hot, then add the omelette batter and tip the pan so it spreads out thinly over the base. Sprinkle some sesame seeds on top and cook for a couple of minutes, then when you see air bubbles appear on the surface, it's time to flip to the other side and cook until just set.

Put the omelette onto a plate, fill with the cabbage mixture and some added spring onion slithers, then fold over the edges. For extra heat, add some chilli sauce or, my favourite, sriracha, if you like!

MAKES 1 LARGE OMELETTE ENOUGH FOR 2 PORTIONS OR DOUBLE FOR ONE OMELETTE EACH

2 tablespoons olive oil
2 garlic cloves, chopped
¼ head of Chinese leaves (stem lettuce), thinly sliced
1 carrot, grated
1 tablespoon medium-heat tamari
1 tablespoon sesame seeds
1 teaspoon sesame oil
1 spring onion (scallion), green and all, thinly sliced, plus extra to serve
chilli sauce or sriracha, to serve (optional)

FOR THE OMELETTE

1 tablespoon olive oil
60 g (2 oz/½ cup) chickpea (gram) flour
⅛ teaspoon bicarbonate of soda (baking soda)
1 teaspoon apple cider vinegar
125 ml (4 fl oz/½ cup) water
1 tablespoon sesame seeds

BOOSTER

sesame oil

SAND-WICHES SALAD & SOUP

I have dedicated a whole chapter to these incredibly simple foods that so easily become my go-to options during busy times. Many of them can be made in larger batches, kept handy in the fridge and easily packed into lunch boxes. All are made from scratch, are easy to put together and totally satisfying.

02

BATCH COOKABLE

FREEZABLE

LASTS FOR 2+ DAYS IN THE FRIDGE

NUT-FREE

TOKYO HUMMUS SANDWICH

Believe it or not, Japan has a bit of a sandwich culture – although perhaps not quite the type you may be thinking of. When visiting Tokyo I had at least one of these rice parcels *(onigirazu)* a day filled with different ingredients each time. This is inspired by my friend Sara Kiyo Popowa, aka Shisodelicious.

Make sure you have cooked the sushi rice according to the packet instructions, and leave it to cool. To make the hummus, blitz all the ingredients together until you get a nice smooth texture. Store in a glass jar and set aside until later.

Heat the olive oil in a frying pan (skillet) over a medium heat. Add the kale and let it wilt, adding the tamari. Give it a stir for a few minutes and set aside.

Now for the assembly. Lay a piece of baking parchment on the work surface and top with a sheet of nori. Thinly spread a quarter of the cooked rice on top of the nori. Place a generous dollop of your Tokyo hummus, some wilted tamari kale and some pickled ginger on top, then another quarter of the rice on top of the other ingredients. Fold two sides of the seaweed to the middle, then the remaining two sides to close the sandwich. Repeat with the remaining ingredients. Wrap the sandwiches in the baking parchment and leave it in the fridge for a little bit to let the seaweed settle. Cut the sandwiches in half and eat straight away or take with you to work, scattering over the spring onions and extra black sesame seeds to serve.

MAKES 4 SANDWICHES

240 g (8½ oz/2 cups) precooked sushi rice
1 tablespoon olive oil
1 handful of kale
1 teaspoon tamari
2 nori sheets
1 spring onion (scallion), green and all, chopped
pickled ginger

FOR THE HUMMUS

240 g (8½ oz/1 cup) drained tinned chickpeas (garbanzos)
juice of 1 lemon
120 ml (4 fl oz/½ cup) light roast tahini (sesame paste)
1 garlic clove
30 g (1 oz/scant ¼ cup) black sesame seeds, plus extra to serve
60 ml (2 fl oz/¼ cup) water

BATCH COOKABLE

FREEZABLE

+3 DAYS

LASTS FOR 3+ DAYS IN THE FRIDGE

NUT-FREE

FAUX TUNA MELT TOASTIE

I have always loved sandwich fillers, especially creamy mayonnaise ones, and that will not change anytime soon. So for completely selfish reasons this faux tuna recipe came about and I am so happy I am able to share it with you.

Start off by putting the artichokes, cornichons, carrot, mayonnaise, mustard, lemon juice and dill in a bowl, season with salt and pepper and give it a good mix. Brush both sides of the bread with oil, then spread two slices with the mix, put a slice of plant cheese on top and seal the sandwich with the other slices of bread.

Get a frying pan (skillet) nice and hot with a splash of olive oil. Put your sandwiches in the pan and fry for about 5 minutes until a nice crispy brown on the base before flipping and browning the other side. Place on a cutting board and slice in the middle. Eat immediately but carefully so you don't burn your mouth.

MAKES 4 TOASTIES

240 g (8½ oz) drained tinned artichokes, chopped
4 cornichons, chopped
1 carrot, grated
4 tablespoons Plant Mayo (see page 144) or shop-bought
1 tablespoon Dijon mustard
juice of ½ lemon
1 tablespoon chopped dill
4 slices of sourdough or good-quality gluten-free bread
olive oil, for brushing
2 pieces of melty plant cheese (optional)
salt and freshly cracked black pepper

The Ultimate BLT p. 49

Egg Sandwich p. 48

BATCH COOKABLE

FREEZABLE

LASTS FOR 3+ DAYS IN THE FRIDGE

NUT-FREE

EGG SANDWICH

I have cracked it, literally! This is really good and if you have been a vegan for a long time and you miss eggs, you will hopefully thank me. If you are new to the whole vegan thing and thought you could not live without eggs, then let's hope this will do the trick!

Let's start off with the vegan egg. Put all the ingredients in a bowl and mix well. Heat a medium-sized non-stick frying pan (skillet) over a medium heat and add a splash of olive oil. Pour in the egg batter and allow it to spread in the pan. Once you see bubbles on the surface, after about 5 minutes, flip on to the other side and cook for another couple of minutes, it goes quick! Once the omelette is done, place on a plate and let it cool down.

Put the rest of the filling ingredients in a bowl and give it a good mix. Once your omelette has cooled down, which should be pretty quick, slice it into small chunks (as you would with an egg), add to the bowl and give it a good mix.

Now toast the bread. Put a handful of watercress and a generous amount of egg filler on one slice of toast and seal with the second. Repeat for the second sandwich, place on a chopping board and slice through the middle. Eat straight away while it is still super-fresh or take to work.

MAKES 4 SANDWICHES

4 slices of sourdough
    or good-quality gluten-free toast
1 handful of watercress

FOR THE VEGAN EGG

60 g (2 oz/½ cup) chickpea
    (gram) flour
⅛ teaspoon bicarbonate of soda
    (baking soda)
1 teaspoon apple cider vinegar
120 ml (4 fl oz/½ cup) water
olive oil, for frying

FOR THE FILLING

4 tablespoons Plant Mayo
    (see page 144) or shop-bought
1 tablespoon capers (baby
    capers), chopped
1 tablespoon snipped chives
1 teaspoon Dijon mustard
juice of ½ lemon
salt and freshly cracked
    black pepper

BATCH COOKABLE

FREEZABLE

+3 DAYS

LASTS FOR 3+ DAYS IN THE FRIDGE

NUT-FREE

THE ULTIMATE BLT

Spicy, fresh, crunchy and absolutely delicious. For those of you with reservations about tofu – and I am one – be reassured that done right it can be yummy, especially sandwiched between crisp veggies and generous amounts of mayonnaise. Buy GMO-free tofu if you can.

Preheat the oven to 180°C (350°F/Gas 4) and line a baking (cookie) tray with baking parchment.

Cut the tofu into 6 slices and make sure you pat the slices dry with some paper towels so they are nice and dry. Put the marinade ingredients in a small bowl and stir until the sugar has dissolved. Place the tofu slices on the prepared baking sheet and brush evenly with the marinade on both sides, then put in the oven for 10 minutes. Check that they are nice and crisp, then turn them over and return them to the oven for a further 10 minutes until brown.

While the tofu is browning, soak the onion in the apple cider vinegar and brown sugar to make a quick pickle.

Now let's put this bad boy together by toasting the bread and adding a slathering of mayonnaise, then a lettuce leaf, tomato slice, tofu and quick pickled onions. Seal the sandwich with another piece of toast that has a thin layer of mayonnaise on the inside to sandwich better.

Place on a chopping board, cut through the middle and devour. Make sure no one is around, as this is not the sexiest of sandwiches to eat, but certainly one of the tastiest.

MAKES 4 SANDWICHES

140 g (4¾ oz) GMO-free, extra-firm or smoked tofu
4 slices of sourdough or good-quality gluten-free bread
2 tablespoons Plant Mayo (see page 144) or shop-bought
4 little gem (bibb) lettuce leaves
1 tomato, sliced

FOR THE MARINADE

2 tablespoons tamari
½ teaspoon brown sugar
1 tablespoon olive oil
1 teaspoon barbecue spice mix

FOR THE ONION PICKLE

½ red onion, thinly sliced
1 tablespoon apple cider vinegar
sprinkle of brown sugar

BATCH COOKABLE

FREEZABLE

+3 DAYS

LASTS FOR 3+ DAYS IN THE FRIDGE

NUT-FREE

HERBY QUINOA TABBOULEH

There are hundreds of quinoa and veggie recipes out there, but none as good as this one. This version focuses on being plant and herb heavy with added quinoa instead of the other way around. It's perfect as a lunch box or fridge staple.

Make sure you have your precooked quinoa ready, according to the packet instructions, and you have allowed it to cool.

Slice and dice all the veggies into small cubes (less than 1 cm/½ in) and put them in a bowl with the herbs. Stir well. Add the remaining ingredients and gently toss again. This is a great salad to take along to work or have ready-made waiting for you in the fridge after a long day. Great scooped with baby gem, on a bed of hummus or simply scooped up with bread.

MAKES 2 PORTIONS

240 g (8½ oz/2½ cups) precooked
　quinoa
1 yellow (bell) pepper
1 red (bell) pepper
1 tomato, deseeded
½ red onion
1 handful of parsley, chopped
1 handful of mint, chopped
juice of 1 lemon
2 tablespoons olive oil
1 tablespoon allspice
salt and freshly cracked
　black pepper
little gem (bibb) lettuce leaves
　to scoop it all up with
hummus (shop bought or make
　your own, see page 42)

BATCH COOKABLE

FREEZABLE

+4
DAYS

**LASTS FOR
4+ DAYS IN
THE FRIDGE**

THE BEST BURGER YOU WILL EVER EAT

Don't be afraid of the ingredients list on this recipe – I know it seems long, but these are well worth making and cook beautifully on the grill (broiler) so are perfect to take along to barbecues. This is the burger (with improvements) from *Happy Food*. They freeze really well, and last a good 4–5 days in the fridge and can be made fresh.

Heat the oil in a large frying pan (skillet) and fry the leek, mushrooms, thyme, chopped tofu and kale for about 5 minutes. Then add the mustard, tamari, and half of the drained black beans and give it a good stir. Transfer the mixture to a blender and pulse a few times but make sure the mixture is still chunky and has bite. Take the contents of the blender and scoop into a bowl and add the rest of the black beans, the oat bran, rice and chopped nuts and give it a good mix. Shape the burger mixture into patties and let them rest in the fridge if you are grilling (broiling) them. If you are pan frying them you can fry them off straight away. I like dipping them into chickpea flour before but it's just an option.

For the burger dressing, mix all the ingredients in a bowl and set aside.

Fry the patties for 4–5 minutes on each side until lovely and crisp.

Choose your burger toppings, add a pattie and some sliced tomatoes, red onion and lettuce to your burger bread and a generous dollop of burger dressing and enjoy!

MAKES 4–6 PATTIES

½ leek, green and all, chopped
5 mushrooms, chopped
30 g (1 oz) thyme leaves
140 g (4¾ oz) GMO-free firm tofu,
   chopped
1 handful of kale
1 tablespoon Dijon mustard
2 tablespoons tamari
240 g (8½ oz) drained tinned
   black beans
3 tablespoons oat bran
2 tablespoons precooked
   brown rice
2 tablespoons chopped hazelnuts
   (filberts) or walnuts
40 g (1½ oz/generous ⅓ cup)
   chickpea (gram) flour (optional)
olive oil, for frying
sliced tomatoes, red onion and
   lettuce, to serve
burger buns, to serve

FOR THE BURGER DRESSING

4 tablespoons Plant Mayo
   (see page 144) or shop-bought
1 teaspoon tomato ketchup
1 tablespoon chopped cornichons
salt and freshly cracked
   black pepper
1 pinch of cayenne

BATCH COOKABLE

NUT-FREE

CRISP FENNEL & ORANGE BROCCOLI SALAD

This a really nice fresh salad that is a great addition to any of the meals in this book or can be eaten on its own. The focus here is winter veggies and including them in new and different ways.

Bring a large saucepan of water to the boil, add the broccoli and flash boil for 5 minutes, then drain and cool under cold water. Once cooled, put in a blender with the coconut cream and blitz until you have a lovely purée. Season with salt and pepper to taste, if you like. Pour onto a serving plate.

Shave the fennel, cucumber and onion into a bowl using a mandoline or peeler, or slice very thinly. Add the orange and avocado. Mix together all the dressing ingredients, and toss with the vegetables. Spoon onto the bed of broccoli purée, top with fennel fronds and eat immediately! If you let the salad sit, it will quickly become soggy.

MAKES 2 PORTIONS

1 head of broccoli, chopped
   from root to top
1 tablespoon coconut cream
salt and freshly cracked
   black pepper

FOR THE WINTER VEGGIES

½ head of fennel, fronds reserved
½ cucumber
¼ red onion
½ orange, sliced in moons
1 avocado, peeled, pitted
   and sliced
1–2 small green and red chicory,
   shredded

FOR THE DRESSING

2 tablespoons olive oil
juice of ½ lemon
½ teaspoon Dijon mustard
1 splash of maple syrup
salt and freshly cracked
   black pepper

BOOSTERS

hemp hearts
chopped nuts

BATCH COOKABLE

FREEZABLE

LASTS FOR 3+ DAYS IN THE FRIDGE

LUNCH BOX PASTA SALAD

You can't beat a pasta salad, especially one that is boosted with plant power to get you through a long day. Also it is time we shine a light on sundried tomato pesto, less well known than green pesto but equally tasty. Switch up your pasta by using chickpea, buckwheat or other types of pasta.

Start off by boiling the pasta as per the packet instructions. Make sure you have plenty of water if you are using gluten-free pasta and that you keep an eye on it so as to not overcook! Once boiled (about 8 minutes), drain, drizzle with a little olive oil and set aside.

Prepare the pesto by putting all the ingredients into a blender and blitzing until smooth, then set aside. Prepare all the veggies, including the chickpeas (garbanzos), and put everything in a bowl with generous tablespoons of pesto so that it covers the pasta properly. No one likes a dry pasta salad. Give it a taste and if needs extra salt and pepper, go ahead and add some.

MAKES 2 PORTIONS

150 g (5 oz) dried gluten-free penne pasta (or good-quality normal)
¼ onion, sliced
240 g (8½ oz/1 cup) drained tinned chickpeas (garbanzos)
60 g (2 oz) rocket (arugula) leaves
60 g (2 oz) baby spinach leaves
olive oil, for drizzling

FOR THE RED PESTO

140 g (5 oz) jar of sundried tomatoes (save the oil for blending)
20 g (¾ oz/2 tablespoons) hazelnuts (filberts)
1 garlic clove
salt and freshly cracked black pepper

BOOSTERS

hemp hearts
extra herbs, such as basil or parsley

BATCH COOKABLE

NUT-FREE

JAPANESE SOBA NOODLE SOUP

This is not a traditional Japanese soup. It is the Bettina's Kitchen coming home from work, quick-fix soup, and it's delicious.

Heat a little olive oil in a medium-sized pan and fry the shallot for a few minutes until translucent. Add the boiling water and the noodles and bring to a simmer for about 5 minutes. In a small bowl, mix the miso with some water and the ginger, add to the broth and give it a good mix. Cut the pak choy in half and add to the broth, scatter the spring onions on top and serve the soup immediately, topped with the sesame seeds, if using.

MAKES 2 PORTIONS

olive oil, for frying
1 shallot, sliced
1 litre (34 fl oz/4 cups) boiling water
200 g (7 oz) soba noodles
2 tablespoons miso paste
1 thumb-sized piece of ginger
 root, grated
2 pak choy (bok choy), halved
2 spring onions (scallions), green
 and all, sliced
a sprinkle of sesame seeds,
 to serve (optional)

BOOSTER

sesame seed oil

BATCH COOKABLE

FREEZABLE

+2 DAYS

LASTS FOR 2+ DAYS IN THE FRIDGE

QUICK LAKSA

This is a flavour bomb! So many seasonings married together combined with creaminess, veggies, a kick and a squeeze of acidity. The best combination, if you ask me.

Put the rice noodle nests in a large bowl and cover with boiling water from a kettle. Leave to stand.

Put all the base ingredients in a blender and whizz until you have a lovely yellow, creamy base and set aside.

Heat a little olive oil in a large frying pan (skillet) and fry the sliced onion and mushrooms for about 5 minutes until nice and soft. Add the base cream to the pan and gently bring to a simmer. Drain the noodles and add them to the pan with a handful of kale and give it a good mix until it's nice and hot. Season with salt and pepper to taste and serve immediately with some fresh spring onion and coriander.

MAKES 2 PORTIONS

2 rice noodle nests (200 g/7 oz)
olive oil, for frying
1 onion, sliced
4 mushrooms, sliced
1 large handful of kale
salt and freshly cracked
   black pepper
chopped spring onions (scallions)
   or chopped coriander (cilantro)
   leaves, to serve

FOR THE BASE

1 shallot, chopped
½ lime, skinned and chopped
½ chilli
30 g (1 oz/¼ cup) cashews
1 teaspoon coriander seeds
1 teaspoon ground cumin
1 teaspoon turmeric
1 teaspoon sweet paprika
400 ml (13 fl oz/generous 1½ cups)
   coconut milk

BATCH COOKABLE

FREEZABLE

LASTS FOR 3+ DAYS IN THE FRIDGE

NUT-FREE

FIVE-MINUTE PEA SOUP WITH BHAJI PANCAKES

Ridiculously easy, super-tasty and great as a quick dinner after a long day at work, this truly feels like a hug in a bowl – comfort on a high level.

To make the pancakes, heat a little olive oil in a large frying pan (skillet) and fry the onion for about 5 minutes until soft. Add the dates and set aside. Put all the remaining ingredients in a bowl and mix well, then stir in the onion and dates. Reheat the pan, then spoon out your pancakes one by one. There should be enough for four pancakes in total. Once there are small air bubbles on one side, it's time to flip. Set them aside and keep them warm, the soup will be done in no time.

To make the soup, heat a little olive oil in a medium-sized saucepan. Add the peas, from frozen, and the Plant Cream and some salt and pepper and gently heat up. Once heated through, transfer all the ingredients to a blender and blitz until smooth. Serve immediately with your beautiful pancakes and a dollop of yoghurt and fresh herbs for extra zing. Use your pancakes as scoops or dippers.

MAKES 2 PORTIONS

olive oil, for frying
375 g (13 oz/2½ cups) frozen peas
250 ml (8½ fl oz/1 cup) Plant Cream (see page 142)
salt and freshly cracked black pepper

FOR THE PANCAKES

olive oil, for frying
1 red onion, sliced
2–4 medjool dates, torn into pieces
120 g (4 oz/1 cup) buckwheat flour
250 ml (8½ fl oz/1 cup) water
1 pinch of bicarbonate of soda (baking soda)
½ teaspoon baking powder
1 teaspoon yellow curry powder
1 teaspoon salt
plant yoghurt or coriander (cilantro) or parsley leaves, to serve

BOOSTERS

hemp hearts
dash of olive oil

**BATCH
COOKABLE**

FREEZABLE

NUT-FREE

MEXICAN NACHO PLATE

Take 10 minutes out of your time to make this plate of deliciousness, put on a great movie, relax and indulge yourself.

To make the black beans, put the drained beans in a blender with the fajita spice mix, Plant Cream and a pinch of salt and pulse until well mixed. Scoop out onto a plate and spread evenly. Next mash the avocado with the squeeze of lemon and a sprinkle of salt and put on top of the black beans.

To make the salsa, put the tomato halves in a bowl and add the remaining salsa ingredients. Toss gently.

Put a dollop of salsa on the plates, scatter the corn chips around the edges and add some lime wedges for extra zing, if you like. Enjoy straightaway!

MAKES 2 PORTIONS

240 g (8½ oz) drained tinned
 black beans
1 tablespoon fajita spice mix
1 splash of Plant Cream
 (see page 142)
1 avocado, peeled and pitted
1 squeeze of lemon juice
salt
corn chips, to serve
lime wedges, to serve (optional)

FOR THE FRESH SALSA

300 g (10½ oz) cherry tomatoes,
 halved
30 g (1 oz) coriander (cilantro)
 leaves, chopped
½ shallot, finely chopped
½ chilli, chopped
1 pinch of salt and freshly cracked
 black pepper

BATCH
COOKABLE

FREEZABLE

+3
DAYS

LASTS FOR
3+ DAYS IN
THE FRIDGE

NUT-FREE

FRIDGE RAID SOUP

This is my once-a-week fridge raid soup. It uses up any leftover sad veggies you have in your fridge and is super-quick! I like chopping my vegetables nice and chunky for this dish.

Heat a little olive oil in a large pan and fry all the veggies for 5–10 minutes until soft, stirring occasionally. Add the spices and give it a good stir. Once slightly charred and softened, add the boiling water, butter beans and stock cube and let it simmer for 10–15 minutes until you have the desired texture for your veggies. I love mine with a slight bite so I let the soup cook less. Enjoy with a lovely chunk of bread and some fresh herbs and a drizzle of good olive oil.

MAKES 2 PORTIONS

olive oil, for frying and drizzling
about 300 g (10 oz) mixed
    vegetables, chopped
5 black peppercorns
2 bay leaves
1 tablespoon harissa
1 tablespoon sweet paprika
1 litre (34 fl oz/4 cups) boiling water
240 g (8½ oz) drained tinned
    butter (lima) beans
1 vegan stock cube
bread, to serve
herbs such as basil, thyme or sage
    leaves, to serve

BOOSTER

hemp hearts

**BATCH
COOKABLE**

FREEZABLE

+3
DAYS

**LASTS FOR
3+ DAYS IN
THE FRIDGE**

NUT-FREE

BUTTERNUT, COCONUT & GINGER SOUP

It is amazing how something so easy can be so tasty. For some reason this recipe has always been a crowd pleaser and continues to be. You just have to give it a go!

Heat a little olive oil in a large saucepan and fry the onion for about 5 minutes with the turmeric and a pinch of black pepper. Add the squash and fry for another 10 minutes until the squash becomes semi soft, then add the stock, bring to the boil and let it simmer for 5 minutes. Finally add the ginger, coconut milk, salt and pepper to taste and blitz in a blender until nice and smooth. Serve immediately with a dash of coconut cream or coriander and parsley leaves.

MAKES 2 PORTIONS

olive oil, for frying
½ onion, sliced
1 teaspoon turmeric
1 butternut squash, peeled
  and finely diced
100 ml (3½ fl oz/scant ½ cup)
  vegan stock
1 large thumb-sized piece of ginger
  root, grated, or 1 tablespoon
  ground ginger
400 ml (13 fl oz/generous 1½ cups)
  coconut milk
salt and freshly cracked
  black pepper
coconut cream or coriander
  (cilantro) or parsley leaves,
  to serve

BOOSTERS

hemp hearts
pumpkin seeds
olive oil or flaxseed oil

**BATCH
COOKABLE**

NUT-FREE

BROTH & GREENS

This is my go-to meal when I am feeling under the weather, or if it's drizzly and cold outside. I also enjoy this meal for breakfast, especially after I return from travelling in Asia, where they often serve brothy breakfasts.

Heat a little olive oil in a large saucepan, add the onion, garlic and five-spice and fry gently for about 5 minutes. Add the cinnamon stick and stock and bring to a simmer. Once simmering, add the pak choy, the tenderstem broccoli and kale. Simmer for a few more minutes. Lastly add the precooked rice, freshly grated ginger and tamari.

Serve immediately with your favourite toppings. I love sriracha, spring onions or chilli for extra kick.

MAKES 2 PORTIONS

olive oil, for frying
½ onion, sliced
3 garlic cloves, chopped
1 teaspoon five-spice
1 cinnamon stick
500 ml (17 fl oz/2 cups) vegan stock
2 pak choy (bok choy), cut in half
100 g (3½ oz) tenderstem broccoli,
    cut in bite-sized pieces
1 handful of kale
260 g (9½ oz/1½ cups) precooked
    brown or white rice
1 thumb-sized piece of ginger root,
    freshly grated
1 tablespoon tamari
sriracha hot sauce, chopped chilli
    or spring onions (scallions),
    green and all, chopped, to serve

BOOSTERS

hemp hearts
pumpkin seeds
sesame seeds

ONE-P
& PAN
WOND

We all need quick and simple recipes in our lives. As someone who works full time, I can appreciate that time is of the essence. This is the solution to cooking from scratch, but with plenty of goodness all cooked in one pan or pot. The toppings and boosters are here to entice your taste buds, and make it as easy or as complicated as you want it to be.

OT

ERS

03

**BATCH
COOKABLE**

NUT-FREE

VEGGIE FRITTERS WITH SWEET CHILLI DIP

These colourful little beauties are crispy on the outside and soft on the inside. They pack a spice punch and hit the spot!

Mix the flour, bicarbonate of soda, cider vinegar and water in a large mixing bowl and leave to stand. Squeeze the courgette of excess liquid and add to the vegan egg mix with the rest of the ingredients.

Heat a splash of olive oil in a large frying pan (skillet) and spoon out the fritters four at a time. I then gently press down the fritters with a saucepan lid that is smaller than the pan. Fry for 3–5 minutes on each side until golden brown and crisp. Repeat with the rest of the mixture and serve immediately with chilli jam, a salad, and some sesame seeds to boost, if you like.

**MAKES 6 FRITTERS,
ENOUGH FOR 3 PORTIONS**

60 g (2 oz/½ cup) chickpea
   (gram) flour
⅛ teaspoon bicarbonate of soda
   (baking soda)
1 teaspoon apple cider vinegar
125 ml (4 fl oz/½ cup) water
olive oil, for frying

FOR THE FILLING

¼ courgette (zucchini), cut into
   ribbons with a vegetable peeler
1 teaspoon Jamaican jerk spice
1 red or yellow (bell) pepper,
   thinly sliced
½ carrot, cut into ribbons
1 spring onion (scallion),
   green and all, sliced
1 bunch of rainbow chard
   or kale, chopped
salt and freshly cracked
   black pepper
chilli jam and vegetables
   or green salad, to serve

BOOSTERS

sesame seeds
hemp hearts

BATCH COOKABLE

FREEZABLE

LASTS FOR 3+ DAYS IN THE FRIDGE

NUT-FREE

RED LENTIL DHAL & TANDOORI CHICKPEAS

Comforting and hearty with added crunch, this is perfect for large batch cooking and to take away for lunch on a drizzly day. One of my favourites. Strictly speaking, this requires a baking sheet as well as a frying pan, but roasting chickpeas is so simple, and makes a huge difference to the flavour and texture.

Preheat the oven to 180°C (350°F/Gas 4) and line a baking (cookie) sheet with baking parchment.

To cook the crispy chickpeas, put the drained chickpeas in a bowl with the spice mix and olive oil and mix so they are well coated. Scatter them on the prepared sheet and pop in the oven for about 20 minutes until golden and crunchy.

Meanwhile, heat a little olive oil In a large frying pan (skillet) and fry the leek, garlic, dates and spices for a good 5–10 minutes until soft. Add the lentils and boiling water and simmer for about 15 minutes until the water has been absorbed. Add the coconut milk and season with salt and pepper to taste, then simmer for another 10 minutes until the lentils have a lovely creamy texture. Once it's ready, ladle in a handful of spinach and top off with crispy chickpeas, a dollop of plant yoghurt and toasted sourdough for scooping.

MAKES 2 PORTIONS

olive oil, for cooking
1 leek, green and all, chopped
3 garlic cloves, chopped
2 medjool dates, torn into pieces
1 tablespoon turmeric
1 teaspoon fenugreek seeds
100 g (3½ oz/⅓ cup) red lentils
250 ml (8½ fl oz/1 cup) boiling water
400 ml (13 fl oz/generous 1½ cups)
    coconut milk
1 large handful of fresh spinach
salt and freshly cracked
    black pepper
plant yoghurt, to serve
sourdough bread, toasted,
    to serve

FOR THE CRISPY CHICKPEAS

240 g (8½ oz/1 cup) drained tinned
    chickpeas (garbanzos)
1 tablespoon tandoori spice mix
1 tablespoon olive oil

BATCH COOKABLE

FREEZABLE

LASTS FOR 3+ DAYS IN THE FRIDGE

CREAMY SATAY NOODLES WITH SALT & PEPPER FRIED TOFU

One of my most popular easy recipes. I love both creamy dishes and noodles, so this is a match made in heaven on a plate.

Switch on the kettle and put your rice noodle nests in a bowl. Cover with boiling water and set aside.

Heat a generous amount of olive oil in a small pan, then add the tofu and season with salt and pepper to taste. Fry over a high heat until crispy on the outside, then set aside.

In the same pan, heat a generous amount of olive oil and add the onion and garlic. Fry until soft, then add the peanut butter, tamari and a sprinkle of brown sugar in a large pan and mix on low heat until you have a lovely creamy consistency. Add the grated carrots and drained rice noodles and mix well until the noodles are covered in sauce. Ladle into bowls and top with the tofu and sprinkles of sesame seeds and spring onion. Serve immediately.

MAKES 2 PORTIONS

200 g (7 oz) rice noodle nests
olive oil, for frying
140 g (5 oz) GMO-free firm
    or smoked tofu, cut lengthways
    into finger shapes
½ yellow onion, sliced
2 garlic cloves, sliced
4 tablespoons peanut butter
2 tablespoons tamari
1 pinch of brown sugar
2 carrots, grated
salt and freshly cracked
    black pepper
sesame seeds and spring onions
    (scallions), green and all,
    chopped, to serve

BATCH COOKABLE

FREEZABLE

LASTS FOR 1+ DAY IN THE FRIDGE

CARBONARA WITH ROASTED BROCCOLI & PEAS

This is my go-to comfort recipe. Once you have tried this it will be on repeat, I promise.

Heat a little olive oil in a frying pan (skillet) and fry the shallot over a medium heat for about 5 minutes until nice and soft. Add the peas and tenderstem broccoli, and season with salt and pepper to taste. Stir gently and leave to warm through.

Bring a large saucepan of water to the boil, add the pasta and cook for 8 minutes until the pasta is al dente. While the pasta is boiling, make the cream sauce by putting the cashews and water in a blender until you get a silky smooth mixture.

When the pasta is al dente, drain the pasta and return it to the pan. Add the sauce to the pan and stir with a pair of tongs until the sauce is fully incorporated with the pasta. Finally top of with a generous helping of the Nut-free Plant Parmesan and a sprinkling of herbs and eat straight away.

MAKES 2 PORTIONS

olive oil, for frying
1 shallot, chopped
125 g (4 oz/1 cup) frozen peas
125 g (4 oz) tenderstem broccoli, cut into bite-sized pieces
salt and freshly cracked black pepper
200 g (7 oz) good-quality spaghetti, gluten-free or normal

FOR THE CREAM SAUCE

150 g (5 oz/1 cup) pre-soaked cashews (soaked for 2 hours, or 20 minutes in hot water)
375 ml (12½ fl oz/generous 1½ cups) water
Nut-free Plant Parmesan (see page 144) and chopped herbs of choice, to serve

**BATCH
COOKABLE**

FREEZABLE

**+3
DAYS**

**LASTS FOR
3+ DAYS IN
THE FRIDGE**

NUT-FREE

EXPRESS LEEK & BEAN RED CURRY

This is an instant dinner made in minutes and I bet this is quicker than ordering take away. I dare you! Why not make your own curry paste, then save what's left over to use over the following weeks.

If you are going to make your own curry paste, put all the ingredients in a blender and blitz until smooth. Scoop into an airtight jar and you can store it in the fridge for a few weeks. Make sure to cover in some olive oil.

Start the curry by heating the olive oil in a large frying pan (skillet) and frying the leeks and garlic for 5–10 minutes until soft. Then add your butter beans and tomatoes and give it a stir. Add the curry paste and coconut milk and simmer for 5 minutes. Add a large handful of fresh spinach just before serving and eat with steamed rice or quinoa, topped off with fresh herbs.

MAKES 2 PORTIONS

olive oil, for frying
1 leek, green and all, chopped
1 garlic clove, chopped
400 g (14 oz) tin of butter (lima)
   beans, drained
1 large tomato, diced
2 tablespoons red curry paste
   (see below or use shop-bought)
60 ml (2 fl oz/¼ cup) coconut milk
1 handful of fresh spinach leaves
rice or quinoa and herbs of your
   choice, to serve

RED CURRY PASTE

1 red chilli, deseeded
1 shallot, diced
2 garlic cloves
1 lemongrass, stem chopped
1 thumb-sized piece of galangal
60 ml (2 fl oz/¼ cup) olive oil

ZANZIBAR POTATOES & SPINACH

BATCH COOKABLE

FREEZABLE

LASTS FOR 3+ DAYS IN THE FRIDGE

NUT-FREE

Spice up your life and your dishes. I love potatoes and this version is delicious. It all goes into one pot and you're sorted!

Heat a little olive oil in a large pan and fry the onion, garlic, spices and diced potato for a good 10 minutes until the onion and potato start to soften. Put the tomatoes and plant cream in a blender and blitz to a smooth sauce. Add to the pan with the beans, season with salt and pepper to taste and simmer for another 10–15 minutes. I love adding a handful of kale right at the end and letting it wilt down just before eating.

MAKES 2 PORTIONS

olive oil, for frying
1 red onion, sliced
3 garlic cloves, sliced
½ teaspoon ground cumin
½ teaspoon ground cinnamon
½ teaspoon sweet paprika
sprinkle of chilli (hot pepper) flakes
1 large sweet potato, peeled and diced
2 tomatoes
80 ml (3 fl oz/⅓ cup) Plant Cream (see page 142)
400 g (14 oz) tin of brown beans, drained
1 handful of kale or spinach
salt and freshly cracked black pepper

BOOSTERS

toasted nuts
herbs of your choice

RAINBOW CURRY RICE & VEGGIES

This is probably my favourite meal in the book. It sounds silly-simple, and it is. But there is something very comforting about it that makes me come back to it again and again.

Heat a little olive oil in a large frying pan (skillet) and fry the leek for 5 minutes until soft. Add the other veggies and the curry powder and cook for another 5–10 minutes on simmer. Season with salt and pepper to taste. Add the coconut milk, cherry tomatoes and cooked rice and heat through. This dish has a soup-like consistency. It is like a wet curry dish and works well with a herb salad. Eat while piping hot.

MAKES 2 PORTIONS

olive oil, for frying
1 leek, green and all, chopped
1 carrot, chopped
½ red (bell) pepper, chopped
100 g (3½ oz) sugar snap peas
½ courgette (zucchini), chopped
1 tablespoon yellow curry powder
400 ml (13 fl oz/generous 1½ cups)
   coconut milk
1 handful of cherry tomatoes,
   halved
60 g (2 oz/scant ½ cup)
   precooked rice
salt and freshly cracked
   black pepper
herb salad, to serve
dollop of coconut yoghurt,
   to serve

BATCH COOKABLE

FREEZABLE

LASTS FOR 2+ DAYS IN THE FRIDGE

NUT-FREE

BUTTER BEAN BUBBLE & SQUEAK

This take on a classic is made with beans for extra protein as well as added texture. Great to make beforehand and have handy as a super-quick dinner.

Heat a splash of olive oil in a medium-sized frying pan (skillet) – I like to use a cast iron one – and fry the onions and cabbage for 5–10 minutes until soft and charred. Add the tamari and mustard and stir. Pour the mixture into a blender, add half the butter beans and blitz. Return the mixture to the pan with the remaining whole beans and the cornflour, and season with salt and pepper to taste. Put the pan on a medium heat and press down the mixture as you would a frittata. Add some extra olive oil if needed. Finish off under the grill (broiler) or in a hot oven for 5–10 minutes until charred.

Meanwhile, mix together the yoghurt sauce ingredients ready to serve with the bubble and squeak and some fresh greens.

MAKES 2 PORTIONS

olive oil, for frying
2 spring onions (scallions),
    green and all, chopped
¼ green cabbage, thinly sliced
1 tablespoon tamari
½ teaspoon Dijon mustard
400 g (14 oz) tin of butter (lima)
    beans, drained
1 tablespoon cornflour
    (cornstarch)
salt and freshly cracked
    black pepper
fresh green vegetables, to serve

FOR THE YOGHURT SAUCE
250 ml (8½ fl oz/1 cup) plant
    yoghurt (oat, coconut, soy)
a squeeze of lemon juice
1 tablespoon capers (baby capers)
½ shallot, finely diced

BATCH COOKABLE

FREEZABLE

LASTS FOR 3+ DAYS IN THE FRIDGE

NUT-FREE

SPICY RED LENTIL & QUINOA POT

A protein boost in the form of a deliciously quick, one-pot fix!
Easy to make and even easier to eat.

Heat a little olive oil in a large frying pan (skillet) and fry the onion, garlic, carrot and spices for 5 minutes until the onion is brown and the carrot soft. Add the chopped cavolo nero, the red lentils and quinoa, cover with the passata and bring to a simmer. Season with salt and pepper to taste and leave to simmer under a lid for about 10–15 minutes until the quinoa and lentils are tender. Serve with a dollop of yoghurt to take the edge off the spice.

MAKES 2 PORTIONS

olive oil, for frying
½ onion, sliced
2 garlic cloves, sliced
2 carrots, diced
1 tablespoon ground cumin
½ teaspoon cayenne
1 tablespoon turmeric
1 large handful of chopped cavolo
　nero or kale
80 g (3 oz/⅓ cup) red lentils
100 g (3½ oz/½ cup) dry quinoa
400 g (14 oz) passata
　(sieved tomatoes) or tinned
　chopped tomatoes
salt and freshly cracked
　black pepper
dollop of coconut yoghurt, to serve

BOOSTERS

black sesame seeds
hemp hearts
toasted nuts

BATCH COOKABLE

FREEZABLE

LASTS FOR 3+ DAYS IN THE FRIDGE

NUT-FREE

MY ETHIOPIAN RICE & SWEET POTATOES

Don't be afraid of the ingredients list on this bad boy version of Ethiopian rice. Once you have had this dish once, it will become a weekly staple. It's extra good after a day when all the ingredients have settled.

Heat a little olive oil in a large pan and gently fry the spices for a few minutes. Then add the onion and sweet potato and fry for another 5 minutes. Crumble in the stock cube, rice, tomato purée and boiling water and bring it all to a simmer. Season with salt and pepper to taste, cover with a lid and simmer gently for 20–30 minutes. By this time all the water should be absorbed and the dish super nice and fluffy. It's great with a dollop of coconut yoghurt and a sprig of mint.

MAKES 2 PORTIONS

olive oil, for frying
1 teaspoon allspice
2 teaspoons coriander seeds
2 teaspoons cumin seeds
1 teaspoons fenugreek seeds
seeds from 4 cardamom pods
1 onion, sliced
1 large sweet potato, peeled
 and diced
1 vegan stock cube
160 g (5½ oz/¾ cup) basmati rice
1 tablespoon tomato purée (paste)
750 ml (25 fl oz/3 cups) boiling
 water
salt and freshly cracked
 black pepper
coconut yoghurt and a sprig
 of mint, to serve

BOOSTERS

chopped nuts
toasted seeds

**BATCH
COOKABLE**

FREEZABLE

**LASTS FOR
2+ DAYS IN
THE FRIDGE**

NUT-FREE

PASTA E FAGIOLI

The title of this simply means 'Pasta with Beans' in Italian. It's a dish we love eating at our Italian Nonno's house, and this is my plant version of a family favourite.

Heat a little olive oil in a large saucepan and fry the onion and garlic for about 5 minutes until soft. At this point I love adding 2–3 sprigs of rosemary and giving it a good mix. Put half the borlotti beans in a blender with the water and blitz until smooth, then add to the onion and garlic and set aside.

Bring another pan of water to the boil with a pinch of salt. Before adding the pasta, give it a bosh and break it a bit. Nonno Mario does this with his pasta fagioli. Add the broken pasta to the water and boil for a good 8 minutes. Once the pasta is just al dente, transfer 250 ml (8½ fl oz/1 cup) of the pasta water to the bean mixture, add the cooked pasta and give it a good mix and season to taste. Serve the pasta fagioli with some mint, bread and a sprinkling of Nut-free Plant Parmesan.

MAKES 2–3 PORTIONS

olive oil, for frying
1 onion, sliced
2 garlic cloves, chopped
2–3 sprigs of rosemary
240 g (8½ oz) drained tinned
   borlotti beans
200 g (7 oz) dried gluten-free
   penne pasta or good-quality
   normal pasta
250 ml (8½ fl oz/1 cup) water
1 vegan stock cube
salt and freshly ground
   black pepper
fresh bread, mint and Nut-free
   Plant Parmesan (see page 144),
   to serve

**BATCH
COOKABLE**

NUT-FREE

KIMCHI FRIED WILD RICE

My love of kimchi has been long and loyal, and so is my love
for South Korea, which I have visited on numerous occasions.
I hope you love this dish as much as I do.

Precook the wild rice mix according to the packet instructions and set aside.
Heat up a little olive oil in a large pan and add the kimchi and fry for
5 minutes. Add the cooked wild rice mix, give it a stir until warmed through,
and add the baby spinach and wilt. Mix well and serve straight away
with spring onions and extra sriracha for strength. Add tamari, if you like.

MAKES 2 PORTIONS

250 g (9 oz/1⅔ cups) precooked
   wild rice mix
olive oil, for frying
120 g (4 oz) vegan kimchi, chopped
100 g (3½ oz) baby spinach
sriracha and chopped spring
   onion (scallion), to serve
2 tablespoons tamari (optional),
   to serve

BOOSTERS
sesame seeds
sesame seed oil

**BATCH
COOKABLE**

**LASTS FOR
2+ DAYS IN
THE FRIDGE**

NUT-FREE

GNUDI WITH TOMATO & BASIL

This recipe was inspired by a lovely client who reminded me of my long lost love of gnudi, which, basically, are large pillowy gnocchi. These are totally gluten free. They are also a great way to use up leftover mash or boiled potatoes.

Start off by boiling your potatoes until soft, then drain until dry. In a large bowl, mash the potatoes and add the cornflour, salt and pepper to taste and knead for a good 5–10 minutes until you have a nice dough. Divide up into balls by using a small-size cookie scoop and set aside.

Heat a little olive oil in a pan and fry the onion and garlic until nice and soft. Add a sprinkle of brown sugar, the tomato purée and tomatoes that have been blitzed in a blender and let the sauce simmer for 5 minutes. Finish off with salt, pepper, thyme and basil and set aside.

Bring a large pot to a boil with a teaspoon of salt and gently ladle in the potato gnudi. They will be ready when they come off the bottom of the pan and float up. Once ready, gently add to the saucepan with the tomato sauce and cover. Sprinkle with a few sprigs of fresh basil and eat straight away while still warm. Serve topped with a sprinkling of Nut-free Plant Parmesan.

MAKES 2 PORTIONS

450 g (1 lb) potatoes, peeled
    and chopped
100 g (3½ oz/heaped ¾ cup) fine
    cornflour (cornstarch)
salt and freshly cracked
    black pepper

FOR THE TOMATO SAUCE

olive oil, for frying
½ onion
3 garlic cloves
sprinkle of brown sugar
1 tablespoon tomato purée (paste)
2 large tomatoes, blitzed in a blender
sprig of thyme
basil and Nut-free Plant Parmesan
    (see page 144), to serve

LEAFY GREEN FRIED RICE

We eat this at home regularly. It is also a great one to make a large batch of and bring to work as it's brilliant eaten cold as well as warm.

Have the rice precooked according to the packet instructions.

Heat a splash of olive oil in a large pan, add the leek and fry for about 3–5 minutes until beginning to soften. Add the broccoli and stir for about another 5 minutes until the vegetables are nice and soft. Stir in the precooked rice, tamari, grated ginger, maple syrup and spinach and fry for a few minutes until all is well incorporated. Serve immediately with sprinkles of sesame seeds, fresh coriander and spring onions.

MAKES 2 PORTIONS

300 g (10½ oz/1⅔ cups)
   precooked rice
olive oil, for frying
½ leek, green and all, chopped
200 g (7 oz) tenderstem broccoli
1 tablespoon tamari
thumb-sized piece of ginger root,
   grated
1 teaspoon maple syrup
1 handful of spinach leaves
sesame seeds, to serve
coriander (cilantro) leaves,
   chopped, to serve
spring onions (scallions), green
   and all, chopped, to serve

BATCH COOKABLE

FREEZABLE

LASTS FOR 2+ DAYS IN THE FRIDGE

NUT-FREE

PYTT I PANNA

This is a very typical Swedish dish usually made from leftovers. This is my humble veggie version with everything I love. Dice the vegetables fairly finely so that they all cook quickly and evenly. I like to finish with a couple of slices of beetroot – you can use fresh, vacuum-packed or from a jar.

Heat a splash of olive oil in a large pan and fry the onion for 5 minutes, then add the sweet potato, potato, pepper and carrot and fry for 10–15 minutes, stirring occasionally, until the potatoes are cooked and soft. Season with salt and pepper to taste. Add the chopped herbs and kale and just allow them to wilt into the mixture. Give it all a good stir just before serving. It is best eaten immediately with a slice or two of beetroot on top.

MAKES 2 PORTIONS

olive oil, for frying
½ red onion, diced
1 sweet potato, peeled and diced
1 large potato, peeled and finely diced
½ yellow (bell) pepper
1 carrot, diced
30 g (1 oz) parsley leaves, chopped
15 g (½ oz) thyme leaves, chopped
1 handful of kale, chopped
salt and freshly cracked black pepper
beetroot (beet) slices, to serve

SAVOU
TRAYB

'Make me once, eat and save some for later.' There is something magical about traybakes. Prepare all your ingredients in different shapes and sizes – you can even spice different sections of your tray to your heart's desire; or change the textures so you have some parts crunchy and others with softer texture; and once out of the oven you can dress with sauces, sprinklings of nuts and fresh herbs. Traybakes are so simple, there's no excuse not to give it a go.

04

MIDDLE EASTERN TRAYBAKE

BATCH COOKABLE

FREEZABLE

LASTS FOR 3+ DAYS IN THE FRIDGE

NUT-FREE

I love Middle Eastern flavours, especially on plant foods. The spices and textures give the veggies a different dimension and flair. The secret to this dish is how you cut your veggies so pay attention – I call this 'hedgehogging' and it is the way you would cut a mango. It is perfect for making sure the flavours are really absorbed into the flesh of the vegetables – and they cook more quickly, too.

Preheat the oven to 180°C (350°F/Gas 4) then line a baking pan with baking parchment.

To hedgehog the aubergine, cut it in half lengthways. Cut the flesh of each half lengthways into quarters without cutting through the skin. Then make 10–12 cuts across the flesh to divide the flesh into chunks. Put the aubergine and onion in the prepared pan.

Mix the dressing ingredients in a bowl, then gently brush some over the veggies. Add the butter beans to the bowl with the remaining dressing, toss and add to the baking pan. Pop in the oven for 20–25 minutes until everything is golden brown. The beans should be slightly crunchy and veggies brown and soft. Once done, top with a drizzle of tahini and pomegranate seeds, then serve with rice, quinoa or flatbreads.

MAKES 2 PORTIONS

1 large aubergine (eggplant)
1 red onion, quartered
400 g (14 oz) tin of butter (lima) beans, drained
rice, quinoa or flatbreads, to serve

FOR THE DRESSING

4 tablespoons olive oil
1 tablespoon harissa
1 tablespoon maple syrup
salt and freshly cracked black pepper

FOR THE TOPPINGS

tahini (sesame paste)
pomegranate seeds

BOOSTER

herbs of your choice

BATCH COOKABLE

FREEZABLE

LASTS FOR 3+ DAYS IN THE FRIDGE

NUT-FREE

FILLED PEPPERS & YOGHURT SAUCE

A dish guaranteed to have everyone coming back for seconds with its warming from-the-inside out cosiness. It will become a winter-time family favourite for sure, and great way to use a whole peppers with minimal waste.

Preheat the oven to 180°C (350°F/Gas 4).

With a short knife, carefully cut around the stem of the peppers to make a lid. Scrape out and discard the seeds from the lids and the inside of the peppers. Brush the interior of the peppers and the inside of the lids with olive oil and sprinkle the insides with salt. Set the peppers on a rimmed baking pan lined with baking paper ready to be filled.

Heat a good glug of olive oil in a frying pan (skillet) and fry the shallot and courgette for a few minutes until nice and soft. Add the spices one by one. Add the rice and stock and turn the heat down to a simmer. Let the rice soak up all the liquid for a good 20 minutes, stirring occasionally, and gradually adding a little more water if the mixture is too dry. Season with salt and pepper to taste, if you like. Remove the rice mixture from the heat and use it to fill up the peppers. Add 2 tablespoons of water to each of the four peppers. Put the lids of the peppers on and place in the oven for 30–40 minutes until the rice inside is fully cooked and the peppers are soft to the touch. If unsure, I sometimes switch off the oven at 30 minutes and let the peppers continue to cook in the residual heat.

While the peppers are cooking, make the herbed yoghurt sauce by mixing all the ingredients together well. Set aside in the fridge.

Once your peppers are ready, serve with the lovely tangy cold sauce and a side of freshly steamed green vegetables.

MAKES 2 PORTIONS

4 medium mixed peppers
olive oil, for brushing and frying
1 shallot, diced
1 courgette (zucchini), finely diced
½ teaspoon coriander seeds
½ teaspoon turmeric
1 pinch of chilli powder
140 g (5 oz/⅔ cup) basmati
   or wild rice
250 ml (8½ fl oz/1 cup) vegan stock
60 ml (2 fl oz/¼ cup) water
salt and freshly cracked
   black pepper
steamed green vegetables,
   to serve

FOR THE HERB YOGHURT

½ cucumber, finely diced
250 g (14 oz) plant yoghurt
1 handful of mint, chopped
1 handful of dill, chopped
1 tablespoon capers
   (baby capers), chopped
1 squeeze of lemon juice
¼ shallot, diced

BATCH COOKABLE

FREEZABLE

LASTS FOR 3+ DAYS IN THE FRIDGE

NUT-FREE

CAULIFLOWER STEAKS WITH SWEDE MASH

A hearty dish that lends itself easily as a plant-based alternative to meat. The mash is great and I have served this on several Sundays as a substitute for the traditional roast dinner. Plus it's a brilliant no-waste meal as we are using the whole cauliflower head, including the leaves.

Preheat the oven to 180°C (350°F/Gas 4).

Remove the outer leaves of the cauliflower and save for later. Cut off the bottom stem to create a flat base so you can stand the cauliflower on the cutting board. Use a large knife to cut the cauliflower head into 2–4 steaks. Save any small bits, for frying.

In a small bowl, stir together the turmeric, mustard, salt and pepper. Brush each side of the cauliflower steaks with the mixture. Heat a large frying pan (skillet) with the oil and place the cauliflower steaks flat-side down. Fry until nice and brown, about 5 minutes on each side. Once charred, place the steaks onto a non-stick baking (cookie) sheet and bake in the oven for another 20 minutes. While the steaks are cooking, make the mash.

To make the mash, boil the swede in a large saucepan of water for about 10–15 minutes until soft, then drain. In a heated pan, fry a handful of the cauliflower leaves in a dash of olive oil until crisp, then season with salt and pepper and set aside. Add the boiled swede to a blender with the coconut milk and blitz until you get a beautifully coloured orange mash. Add salt and pepper to taste and stir through. Add the fried off cauliflower leaves to the mash for extra texture and mix in with a spoon.

Serve a generous dollop of mash, top it off with a cauliflower steak.

MAKES 2 PORTIONS

1 large cauliflower head
   with leaves and all
1 tablespoon turmeric
1 tablespoon Dijon mustard
olive oil, for frying
salt and freshly cracked
   black pepper

FOR THE MASH

1 medium swede, peeled and diced
cauliflower leaves, chopped
   (from above)
olive oil, for frying
1–2 tablespoons coconut milk

BOOSTERS

spinach leaves
pomegranate seeds

BATCH COOKABLE

FREEZABLE

LASTS FOR 3+ DAYS IN THE FRIDGE

NUT-FREE

EMMA'S CARROT MASH SHEPHERD'S PIE

This recipe can look a bit long, but I seriously suggest doubling it so you can keep some for later.

Preheat the oven to 180°C (350°F/Gas 4).

Cook the carrot and potato in boiling water for about 10 minutes until soft. Drain and set aside to cool. Mash with a splash of plant cream and salt and pepper to taste.

Heat a generous slug of olive oil in a large saucepan and fry the onion, garlic and tofu, if using, until nice and soft. Add the spices, herbs and lentils and give it a good mix, then add the quinoa and stock, bring to a simmer, then simmer for 5–10 minutes until the lentils are soft. Stir in the passata and season with salt and pepper to taste. Give it a good mix, then set aside.

Now for the assembly. Spoon the quinoa mix into the bottom of a small- to medium-sized oven dish, top with the carrot mash and pop in the oven for a good 20 minutes. Put the oven on grill for 5 minutes before getting the pie out of the oven to get a golden crust, or make sure you use a flameproof dish and flash it under a hot grill (broiler) to finish. Once out of the oven serve with steamed greens or salad.

MAKES 1 SMALL TRAY

4 large carrots, chopped
1 potato, peeled and chopped
1 tablespoon Plant Cream (see page 142), or shop-bought
salt and freshly cracked black pepper

FOR THE FILLING
1 yellow onion, diced
2 garlic cloves
200 g (7 oz) GMO-free smoked tofu, diced (optional)
1 bay leaf
1 teaspoon sweet paprika
1 teaspoon herbes de Provence
30 g (1 oz) thyme leaves, chopped
60 g (2 oz/¼ cup) red lentils
125 g (4 oz/1 cup) quinoa
240 ml (8½ fl oz/1 cup) vegan stock
350 ml (11½ fl oz/1½ cups) passata (sieved tomatoes)
olive oil, for frying
salt and freshly cracked black pepper
steamed greens or salad, to serve

VEGGIE CRUMBLE

Make this once and keep some for later or for a take-away for lunch. This is the perfect batch-cook type of dish that just keeps getting better and better.

Preheat the oven to 200°C (400°F/Gas 6).

Heat the olive oil in a large saucepan over a medium heat and start adding your base vegetables one at a time in the order listed and frying them until they are all soft, stirring occasionally.

While the veggies are frying, prepare the sauce by putting the pepper and tomato in a blender and blending until you get a smooth sauce. Once done, add to the vegetable mix and let it simmer for a further 10 minutes.

Meanwhile, make the crumble topping by putting the ingredients in a blender and pulsing until you get a crumbly texture. Set aside.

To make the basil pesto, put all the ingredients in a blender and blend until you have a lovely, smooth mixture perfect for drizzling. Set aside.

The vegetable mix should now be nice and soft and fully incorporated with the pepper and tomato sauce. Transfer the mixture into an ovenproof dish, top off with the crumble mixture and put into the oven for 30 minutes and cook until the topping is crisp.

Finish with a good drizzle of pesto and serve with a fresh side salad.

MAKES 4–6 PORTIONS

2 tablespoons olive oil
2 small onions, chopped
2 celery stalks, chopped
1 carrot, chopped
1 sweet potato, peeled and chopped
4–5 mushrooms, chopped
1 big tomato, chopped
1 courgette (zucchini), chopped

FOR THE PEPPER & TOMATO SAUCE

1 (bell) pepper, chopped
1 tomato, chopped

FOR THE CRUMBLE

60 g (2 oz/½ cup) chopped walnuts
40 g (1½ oz/¼ cup) rolled oats
1 tablespoon raw pumpkin seeds
1 tablespoon chopped thyme leaves
1 pinch of salt

FOR THE BASIL PESTO

20 g (¾ oz) basil leaves
125 ml (4 fl oz/½ cup) olive oil
60 g (2 oz/¼ cup) pumpkin seeds
1 pinch of salt

BATCH COOKABLE

FREEZABLE

+3 DAYS

LASTS FOR 3+ DAYS IN THE FRIDGE

TWENTY-MINUTE GREEN PASTA BAKE

There is nothing like a good pasta bake. This one is deliciously creamy and is boosted with extra greens.

Preheat the oven to 180°C (350°F/Gas 4).

Cook the pasta in a large pan of boiling water until al dente, according to the directions on the packet. Drain, reserving the water, and set the pasta aside in a large bowl. Use the hot pasta water to blanch the cavolo nero, then drain. Heat the oil and fry the onion and garlic until soft, then add the mushrooms and fry for another minute or so and set aside. Put the cavolo nero in a blender and add the mushroom mixture, plant cream and thyme, and season with salt and pepper to taste. Blitz until you have a lovely green sauce. Add the sauce to the cooked pasta and mix well, then transfer to a medium-sized oven dish.

In a small blender, blitz the topping ingredients, then sprinkle over the pasta and bake in the oven and bake for 20 minutes until nice and golden. Serve straight away with a salad or steamed greens.

MAKES 2 PORTIONS

200 g (7 oz) penne pasta
4 large cavolo nero leaves
1 onion
2 garlic cloves
200 g (7 oz) chestnut mushrooms, stems and all, chopped
250 ml (8½ fl oz/1 cup) Plant Cream (see page 142)
30 g (1 oz) thyme leaves
olive oil, for frying
salt and freshly cracked black pepper
salad or steamed greens, to serve

FOR THE TOPPING

30 g (1 oz/scant ¼ cup) hazelnuts (filberts) or walnuts
1 garlic clove

BATCH COOKABLE

FREEZABLE

LASTS FOR 2+ DAYS IN THE FRIDGE

ROASTED ROOTS & PEANUT SAUCE

This dish is so good. I always enjoy a good peanut sauce and this is a super-lovely version I learnt in Bali, which can be used for so many different meals.

Prepare all the veggies by slicing them lengthways.

Put all the peanut sauce ingredients in a blender with 120 ml (4 fl oz/½ cup) water and blitz until you have a smooth consistency. Marinate all the veggies in the sauce for about 5 minutes while you preheat the oven to 180°C (350°F/Gas 4) and line a baking (cookie) sheet with baking parchment.

Spoon the vegetables and sauce onto the prepared sheet, stir well and put in the oven for 20–30 minutes until the veggies are golden brown and cooked through. Drizzle with a glug of olive, oil, top with fresh watercress and a sprinkling of spring onions and eat straight away!

MAKES 2 PORTIONS

1 carrot
½ celeriac (celery root), peeled
1 large potato, peeled
1 onion, peeled
1 parsnip, peeled

FOR THE PEANUT SAUCE

125 g (4 oz/¾ cup) unsalted roasted peanuts
1 tablespoon tamari
2.5 cm (1 in) piece of ginger root, chopped
¼ chilli, chopped

FOR THE TOPPING

olive oil, for drizzling
100 g (3½ oz) watercress
1 spring onion (scallion), sliced

BOOSTERS

hemp hearts
peanuts
sesame seeds

**BATCH
COOKABLE**

FREEZABLE

**LASTS FOR
3+ DAYS IN
THE FRIDGE**

NUT-FREE

COURGETTES WITH CHICKPEAS

Since I started hedgehogging my veggies before roasting, a whole new flavour world has opened up. The way the marinade and spices can dig into them changes everything!

Preheat the oven to 180°C (350°F/Gas 4) and line a baking (cookie) sheet with baking parchment.

To hedgehog the courgettes, cut them in half lengthways. Cut the flesh of each half lengthways into quarters without cutting through the skin. Then make 8–10 cuts across the flesh to divide the flesh into chunks all still attached to the skin. Put them in a bowl.

Mix the marinade ingredients in a bowl, then gently brush some over the veggies. Add the chickpeas (garbanzos) to the bowl and stir in the remaining marinade. Spoon the chickpeas and courgettes onto the prepared sheet and cook in the oven for 20–30 minutes until all are lovely and golden.

Stir the spinach and herbs into the vegetables, whisk together the dressing ingredients, drizzle over the veggies then serve with sourdough to scoop up all the goodness.

MAKES 2 PORTIONS

4 large courgettes (zucchini)
240 g (8½ oz/1 cup) drained tinned
 chickpeas (garbanzos)
100 g (3½ oz) baby spinach leaves
fresh herbs of your choice,
 to serve (optional)
toasted sourdough, to serve

FOR THE MARINADE

1 tablespoon harissa paste
 (optional)
1 tablespoon maple syrup
½ tablespoon turmeric
4 tablespoons olive oil
salt and freshly cracked
 black pepper
1 garlic clove, grated

FOR THE DRESSING

4–5 tablespoons tahini
 (sesame paste)
salt and freshly cracked
 black pepper

BOOSTER

chopped toasted nuts
hemp hearts

BATCH COOKABLE

FREEZABLE

+2 DAYS

LASTS FOR 2+ DAYS IN THE FRIDGE

NUT-FREE

FULLY-LOADED SWEET POTATOES

I love sweet potatoes! They are super-versatile, tasty, filling and – last but not least – super-tasty.

Preheat the oven to 200°C (400°F/Gas 6) and line a baking (cookie) sheet with baking parchment. Cut the sweet potatoes in half (to cook faster) and lay them on the prepared baking sheet. Cook for 30 minutes or until soft.

Once roasted, scoop out the insides and mash with the Plant Cream, sweetcorn, pepper, red onion and a squeeze of lime. Season with salt and pepper to taste. Spoon back into the skins. Top with a quarter of the avocado on each half, a few coriander leaves and a sprinkling of chilli for kick.

MAKES 2 PORTIONS

2 large sweet potatoes
2 tablespoons Plant Cream
   (see page 142)
60 g (2 oz) sweetcorn
½ red (bell) pepper, finely diced
¼ red onion, finely diced
1 lime, cut into wedges
1 avocado, peeled, pitted
   and sliced
1 tablespoon finely chopped chilli
coriander (cilantro) leaves
salt and freshly cracked
   black pepper

BOOSTERS

hemp hearts
sesame seeds

BATCH COOKABLE

FREEZABLE

LASTS FOR 2+ DAYS IN THE FRIDGE

NUT-FREE

ROASTED SWEDE & CHIMICHURRI

Swede is so underestimated and under used. I remember having it a lot as a kid, especially as a mash. This recipe is a lovely traybake with lots of extra zing!

Preheat the oven to 210°C (410°F/Gas 7). Prepare the swede by peeling it, cutting it in half and slicing into half moons, around 1 cm (½ in) thick. Line a baking (cookie) sheet with baking parchment and arrange the swede on the sheet, then drizzle with olive oil and sprinkle with salt and pepper to taste. Cook in the oven for 20–30 minutes until lovely and golden brown.

While the swede is cooking, prepare the chimichurri by adding all the ingredients to a mini-blender and pulsing. Don't over-blend as you still want a chunky texture. Once the swede is cooked, drizzle with the chimichurri and scatter watercress and baby spinach across the tray. Enjoy with steamed quinoa, sourdough toast or as is.

MAKES 2 PORTIONS

600–800 g (1 lb 5 oz–1 lb 12 oz) swede, cut into moons
2 tablespoons olive oil
1 handful of baby spinach
1 handful of watercress
salt and freshly cracked black pepper

FOR THE CHIMICHURRI

30 g (1 oz) parsley, chopped
30 g (1 oz) coriander (cilantro), chopped
2 garlic cloves
1 shallot, finely diced
½ red chilli
juice of 1 lime
60 ml (2 fl oz/¼ cup) olive oil
salt and freshly cracked black pepper
steamed quinoa or sourdough toast, to serve (optional)

BATCH COOKABLE

FREEZABLE

LASTS FOR 2+ DAYS IN THE FRIDGE

NUT-FREE

ONE-TRAY SUNDAY ROAST WITH SMASHED PEAS

A real crowd pleaser, super colourful, with lots of texture and, first and foremost, a delicious flavour. This was inspired by my friend and fellow foodie, Niki Webster.

Preheat the oven to 200°C (400°F/Gas 6) and line a baking (cookie) sheet with baking parchment.

Prepare all the veggies, remembering that roots take longer to cook, so the thinner you slice, the quicker they will cook. Mix the olive oil, tamari and garlic in a bowl. Place all the veggies except for the kale on the prepared baking sheet and baste with the olive oil mixture. Cook in the oven for 20 minutes then add the kale, then cook for another 10 minutes until tender and golden.

While the veggies are cooking, put the frozen peas into a medium-sized hot pan and heat through with a splash of Plant Cream. Add to a blender and blitz until smooth, then season with salt and pepper to taste and set aside.

To make the herb sauce, put all sauce ingredients in a blender and blitz with some salt and pepper until you have a lovely smooth sauce.

Once the veggies are brown on the outside and soft in the middle, scoop out the smashed peas onto a large serving plate or divide among portions. Take the veggies out of the oven, place on the mash and drizzle with the herby sauce.

MAKES 2–4 PORTIONS

1 potato, peeled
    and sliced lengthways
1–2 carrots (multi coloured
    if possible), sliced lengthways
2 parsnips, peeled
    and sliced lengthways
1 red onion, sliced lengthways
¼ red cabbage, sliced
1 garlic bulb, sliced
1 handful of kale
2 tablespoons olive oil
1 tablespoon tamari
1 garlic clove, grated

FOR THE SMASHED PEAS

800 g (1 lb 12 oz/5 cups)
    frozen peas
1 splash of Plant Cream
    (see page 142)
salt and freshly cracked
    black pepper

FOR THE HERB SAUCE

30 g (1 oz) parsley
½ chilli, deseeded and sliced
2 tablespoons olive oil
1 squeeze of lemon juice
salt and freshly cracked
    black pepper

HERB-CRUSTED PORTOBELLO & CREAMED SPINACH

If I had a favourite way of eating mushrooms, then this version would definitely be on the top of my list.

Preheat the oven to 180°C (350°F/Gas 4) and line a baking (cookie) sheet with baking parchment.

Place the mushrooms gill-side up on the prepared sheet. Put the olive oil, garlic, herbs, walnuts, salt and pepper in a blender and blitz until smooth. Spoon over the mushrooms, then cook in the oven for 15–20 minutes.

While they are cooking, put the plant cream and spinach in a large saucepan over a medium heat for a few moments to wilt the spinach. Season with salt and pepper.

Once the mushrooms are ready, take them out of the oven, toast the bread and place on a plate. Add the wilted spinach and top with two herbed mushrooms on each piece of bread. Enjoy straightaway.

MAKES 2 PORTIONS

4 portobello mushrooms
4–6 tablespoons olive oil
2 garlic cloves
30 g (1 oz) parsley leaves
30 g (1 oz) basil leaves
20 g (¾ oz/scant ¼ cup) walnuts
salt and freshly cracked
   black pepper
toast, to serve

FOR THE CREAMED SPINACH

4 tablespoons Plant Cream
   (see page 142)
125 g (4 oz) spinach leaves

BOOSTERS

chopped toasted nuts
seeds

**BATCH
COOKABLE**

FREEZABLE

NUT-FREE

KOREAN BARBECUE ROASTED BROCCOLI

I have an intense love of Korean flavours and am so happy that I am able to share that love with you. This marinade isn't just great for these broccoli bites, but for literally anything. It keeps well in the fridge.

Preheat the oven to 200°C (400°F/Gas 6).

Put all the barbecue sauce ingredients in a blender and blitz until you have a smooth sauce.

Toss the vegetables in the barbecue sauce and roast in the oven or on the barbecue for about 15 minutes until just tender but still with a bit of bite.

Serve with steamed rice, noodles or quinoa, scatter over the sesame seeds and drizzle with olive oil, if using.

MAKES 2 PORTIONS

1 big head or 2 small heads
   of broccoli, chopped into
   bite-sized pieces
1 large green (bell) pepper,
   sliced lengthways
sesame seeds, for scattering
olive oil, for drizzling (optional)
steamed rice, rice noodles
   or steamed quinoa, to serve

FOR THE KOREAN BARBECUE SAUCE

½ pear
2 tablespoons tamari
1 thumb-size piece of ginger root
2 garlic cloves
1 tablespoon sesame oil
½ red (bell) pepper
1 shallot, sliced

SWEET TOOTH

This is one of the best parts of the book. This is where you can rustle up something sweet in minutes when that craving sets in. This is also where I have come up with clever solutions to maximise taste. Not to mention some of these decadent treats secretly hide the likes of parsnips and chickpeas.

05

**BATCH
COOKABLE**

**+4
DAYS**

**LASTS FOR
4+ DAYS IN
THE FRIDGE**

GRIDDLED PINEAPPLE & CHILLI FLAKES WITH ALMOND WHIP

If you have never had griddled pineapple, then now is definitely the time to try it. The chilli adds a kick and beautifully contrasts with the dreamy almond whip. The cream keeps for 4 days in the fridge but doesn't usually last that long!

To start the almond whip, put the almonds in a bowl, pour over the boiling water, then set aside.

Prepare the pineapple by cutting off the top and bottom, then the sides. Cut in quarters, then remove the hard core in the middle. Slice the flesh into thick moons.

Heat up a griddle pan over a high heat and add the pineapple. Sprinkle a small amount of chilli and tiny bit of salt over them and char the pineapple quickly on both sides.

Meanwhile, pour the almonds and their soaking water into a blender and add the maple syrup and vanilla paste. Blend into a beautiful white, smooth cream. Serve the hot pineapple slices straightaway with a generous dollop of almond whip.

MAKES 2 PORTIONS

1 small pineapple
1 pinch of chilli powder or chilli
    (hot pepper) flakes
1 tiny sprinkle of salt

FOR THE ALMOND WHIP

125 g (4 oz/¾ cup) blanched
    almonds
240 ml (8½ fl oz/1 cup)
    boiling water
1 tablespoon maple syrup
1 teaspoon vanilla paste

BATCH COOKABLE

FREEZABLE

+7
DAYS

**LASTS FOR
+7 DAYS IN
THE FRIDGE**

ALMOND COOKIES

These take just 12 minutes to make and are so versatile – the options are endless. You can top them with a dollop of coconut yoghurt and jam, or some nutella and banana slices, or anything else that takes your fancy. And did I mention that they are my go-to ice cream sandwich cookies?

Line a baking (cookie) sheet with baking parchment.

Put the almond flour in a bowl and blitz with a handheld blender until you have an even finer flour. Add the rest of the ingredients and pulse until everything is well combined. Scoop out the cookies with a small cookie scoop and place on the prepared sheet. Gently push down each cookie with your hands, then pop them in the freezer for 10–15 minutes while you preheat the oven to 180°C (350°F/Gas 4).

Bake in the oven for exactly 12 minutes. Cool on a wire rack before enjoying as they are, with yoghurt and fruit, sandwiched around ice cream, nut butter or a filling of your choice.

MAKES ABOUT 6 COOKIES

160 g (5½ oz/1½ cups) almond flour
90 ml (3 fl oz/scant ½ cup) rice malt syrup
1 teaspoon vanilla paste
60 ml (2 fl oz/¼ cup) coconut oil
½ teaspoon baking powder
1 pinch of ground cinnamon
Two-minute Ice Cream (see page 134), to serve (optional)

BATCH COOKABLE

FREEZABLE

+5 DAYS

LASTS FOR 5+ DAYS IN THE FRIDGE

FIFTEEN-MINUTE FLOURLESS CHOC CHIP BANANA MUFFINS

I don't usually toot my own horn, but these are genius! My daughter and husband love them. They are great as a snack to take away and real winners at bake sales. It's important that the peanut butter is runny/loose, and the coconut oil is melted, otherwise the mixture will become dense.

Preheat the oven to 180°C (350°F/Gas 4) and line a muffin pan with 8 paper cases.

Put all the ingredients into a blender and blitz until you have a beautiful smooth mixture. Scoop the mixture into the 8 muffin cases. Put one or two pieces of chocolate into each muffin along with a slice or two of banana. Bake in the oven for 12–15 minutes. The muffins will be lovely and cooked on the outside but still gooey on the inside. Leave them to cool on a wire rack, then enjoy.

MAKES 8 MUFFINS

240 g (8½ oz/1 cup) drained tinned chickpeas (garbanzos)
60 g (2 oz/⅓ cup) brown or coconut sugar
3 tablespoons maple syrup
3 tablespoons melted coconut oil
60 g (2 oz/¼ cup) runny peanut butter
60 g (2 oz/½ cup) cacao
1 teaspoon vanilla paste
160 ml (5½ fl oz/⅔ cup) Oat Milk (see page 142) or other plant milk
½ teaspoon bicarbonate of soda (baking soda)
1 teaspoon baking powder

FOR THE TOPPING

100 g (3½ oz) dark or milk dairy-free chocolate, chopped
1 banana, sliced

BATCH COOKABLE

FREEZABLE

LASTS FOR +14 DAYS IN THE FRIDGE, ESPECIALLY IF GOING FOR THE AGING

'CHOCOLATE' SALAMI

The first time I had this wonder was in Italy. It was slightly naughtier as it had a dash of rum in it. This is a great little treat to have in your fridge that you can cut slithers off when you are craving something a little decadent.

Put the hazelnuts, cacao, flour, maple syrup and coconut oil into a blender and blitz until all is well combined and is slightly sticky. Take out and put in a small bowl. Add the crushed cookies and torn dates and mix well. Spoon the mixture onto a sheet of baking parchment, shape into a salami, roll up and tighten at both ends. Let it set in the fridge for a few hours or flash freeze in the freezer for 30 minutes. Once set, cut off slivers and enjoy!

MAKES 1 SAUSAGE

60 g (2 oz/½ cup) hazelnuts (filberts)
3 tablespoons cacao
60 g (2 oz/½ cup) almond flour
2 tablespoons maple syrup
1 tablespoon coconut oil
2 Almond Cookies (page 126, or shop-bought, gluten-free if you are coeliac), crushed
2–3 medjool dates, torn into pieces

SCANDI SNOWBALLS

BATCH COOKABLE

FREEZABLE

LASTS FOR +7 DAYS IN THE FRIDGE

NUT-FREE

These are a take on a classic Swedish sweet that I used to make all the time as a kid – my kid now adores them, too. I have kept the original oats as the main ingredient but exchanged the others for plant-based options. These are great stored in the fridge and are super-yummy.

Add all the ingredients except the coconut to a blender and blitz until well combined and slightly sticky. Form 6–8 small balls, then gently roll them in the desiccated coconut and let rest and firm up in the fridge. I usually store these in an airtight container.

MAKES 6–8 BALLS

4–6 tablespoons cacao
200 g (7 oz/2 cups) rolled oats
2–3 tablespoons date syrup
3 tablespoons coconut oil
desiccated (dried shredded)
   coconut, for rolling

BOOSTER

cacao nibs

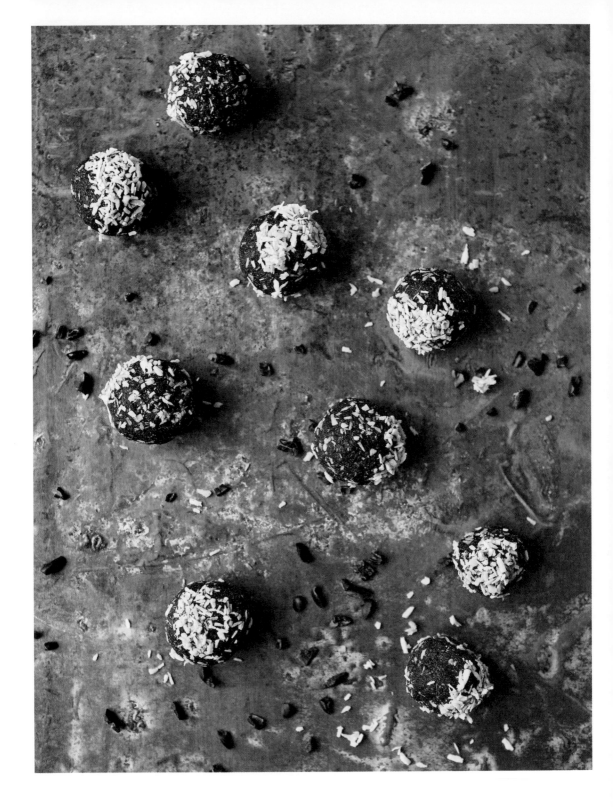

BATCH
COOKABLE

FREEZABLE

NUT-FREE

TWO-MINUTE ICE CREAM

This is a banana-free instant ice cream! Yes, I know that every other instant version out there contains bananas, so let's try something a little bit different.

You will need to have pre-frozen coconut cream in ice cube trays – a small tray should be enough for one portion. Put the coconut cream cubes in a blender along with the other ingredients and blitz until you have instant ice cream. Serve immediately with your choice of toppings – a handful of nuts, seeds, hemp hearts or cacao, or a dollop of nut butter.

MAKES 2–4 PORTIONS

2–4 ice cube trays of frozen
  coconut cream
1 tablespoon maple syrup
1 teaspoon vanilla paste
2–4 tablespoons cacao

BOOSTERS

chopped nuts
seeds
hemp hearts
cacao nibs
nut butter

BATCH
COOKABLE

FREEZABLE

+5
DAYS

LASTS FOR
5+ DAYS IN
THE FRIDGE

TEN-MINUTE THUMBPRINT COOKIES

There is no excuse not to give these cookies a go! Please do me a favour and start making your own homemade cookies rather than buying them. You can thank me later.

Line a baking (cookie) sheet with some baking parchment.

Put the almond and oat flours in a blender and give it a good whizz until both are combined and you have an even finer flour. Add the rest of the ingredients except the jam and pulse until combined. Scoop out 6–8 cookies on to the prepared sheet. Gently create a thumbprint in the middle of each cookie, then put them in the freezer for 10 minutes or in the fridge for about 20 minutes while you preheat the oven to 180°C (350°F/Gas 4).

Put a teaspoon of jam in each thumbprint and bake in the oven for 12–15 minutes until golden. Leave to cool on a wire rack.

MAKES 6–8 COOKIES

125 g (4 oz/1 cup) almond flour
40 g (1½ oz/¼ cup) oat flour
45 g (1¾ oz/¼ cup) brown
  or coconut sugar
90 ml (3 fl oz/⅓ cup) coconut oil
1 teaspoon baking powder
1 pinch of salt
6–8 teaspoons strawberry
  or raspberry jam, or flavour
  of your choice

BATCH
COOKABLE

FREEZABLE

+3
DAYS

LASTS FOR
3+ DAYS IN
THE FRIDGE

NUT-FREE

FIVE-MINUTE FRIED BANANA & CRUMBLE

This is ideal for when you want something sweet and you want it quickly. The added crunchy texture combined with fried banana and a dollop of coconut yoghurt is a match made in heaven.

Put all the crumble ingredients into a bowl and mix together with your fingers until well combined.

Heat a little coconut oil in a medium-sized frying pan (skillet) and fry the bananas flat-side down for 5 minutes until nice and golden. Carefully lift on to serving plates. Spoon the crumble mixture into the same pan and fry for about 5 minutes until nice and crispy, stirring and keeping a close eye that it doesn't catch. Sprinkle the crumble on top of the bananas, add a generous dollop of coconut yoghurt and eat straight away.

MAKES 2 PORTIONS

coconut oil, for frying
2 ripe bananas, peeled and sliced
   lengthways
coconut yoghurt, to serve

FOR THE PAN CRUMBLE

1 tablespoon coconut oil
65 g (2½ oz/⅔ cup) rolled oats
1 teaspoon ground cinnamon
½ teaspoon ground cloves
½ teaspoon ground cardamom
1 teaspoon brown sugar
   or coconut sugar

BATCH
COOKABLE

FREEZABLE

+5
DAYS

LASTS FOR
5+ DAYS IN
THE FRIDGE

PEANUT BUTTER CHOCOLATE POTS

Rich and creamy chocolate mousse pots made dairy-free with thick coconut milk. This is a lovely recipe to make a large batch of and keeps very well in the fridge. Filling and very moreish.

In a medium pan, bring the coconut milk, maple syrup and salt to a gentle boil. Immediately remove from the heat and whisk in the vanilla, followed by the chocolate and nut butter. Whisk until all the ingredients are well mixed together and you have a smooth texture. Divide evenly among individual glass jars or drinking glasses, cool to room temperature, then chill, uncovered, for at least 2 hours in the fridge or pop in the freezer for 20–30 minutes. Sprinkle with nuts, hemp hearts or berries, if you like.

MAKES 4 PORTIONS

400 ml (13 fl oz/generous 1½ cups)
   full-fat coconut milk
1 tablespoon maple syrup
1 pinch of salt
2 teaspoons vanilla paste
125 g (4 oz/¾ cup) dark dairy-free
   chocolate chips or
2 tablespoons your favourite
   nut butter (roasted almond,
   peanut, cashew)

BOOSTERS

chopped nuts
hemp hearts
berries

BATCH COOKABLE

FREEZABLE

LASTS FOR 3+ DAYS IN THE FRIDGE

NUT-FREE

PARSNIP BROWNIE WITH CHOCOLATE MOUSSE TOPPING

Parsnip in a brownie, you say? Parsnips are naturally very sweet and you would be surprised how well they go together. You can keep this cake as simple as you like by just making it into a brownie, or going the whole way and adding a decadent chocolate mousse on top!

Preheat the oven to 180°C (350°F/Gas 4) and grease a 20 cm (8 in) square cake pan with coconut oil.

Boil the parsnip until nice and soft, then drain. Weigh out 130 g (4½ oz) and put in a blender along with all the other brownie ingredients and blend until nice and smooth. Spoon the brownie mixture into the prepared pan and bake for 20 minutes until just firm to the touch. You can serve the cake on its own as simple brownies.

If you decide to go all the way and make the mousse topping, put all the ingredients in a blender and blitz until you have a smooth mixture.

Transfer the cake to a wire rack to cool, then spread the mousse on top and decorate with some berries.

MAKES 6–8 BROWNIES

1 medium parsnip, peeled
60 g (2 oz/½ cup) gluten-free flour mix or buckwheat flour
250 ml (8½ fl oz/1 cup) Oat Milk (see page 142) or other plant milk
75 g (2½ oz/⅓ cup) brown or coconut sugar
6 tablespoons cacao
1 teaspoon baking powder
½ teaspoon bicarbonate of soda (baking soda)
a little coconut oil, for greasing
berries, to serve

FOR THE DECADENT CHOCOLATE MOUSSE

1 large avocado
3 tablespoons maple syrup
6 tablespoons cacao
1 teaspoon vanilla paste
120 ml (4 fl oz/½ cup) coconut milk

138

KEY LIME PIE IN A JAR

BATCH COOKABLE

FREEZABLE

LASTS FOR 3+ DAYS IN THE FRIDGE

A brilliantly simple dessert, this looks good, tastes great and can easily be made beforehand and in large batches. Use seasonal fruit to top it off.

Peel and pit the avocados, chop the flesh and put it in a blender. Add half of the coconut yoghurt, the maple syrup, vanilla paste and lime zest and juice. Blitz until smooth and creamy, then set aside.

To make the crust, add all the ingredients to a food processor and pulse until it has a crumble-like texture.

To assemble, put a layer of crumble in the bottom of 2–4 glass jars, then add a layer of avocado and a few raspberries. Repeat the layers, finishing with a dollop of yoghurt and few raspberries.

MAKES 2–4 PORTIONS

2 avocados
200 g (7 oz) coconut yoghurt
2 tablespoons maple syrup
1 teaspoon vanilla paste
zest and juice of 4 limes
1 handful of raspberries

FOR THE CRUST

100 g (3½ oz/1 cup) ground almonds
25 g (¾ oz/scant ¼ cup) raw, shelled pistachios
25 g (¾ oz/¼ cup) desiccated (dried shredded) coconut
2 tablespoons coconut oil
3 medjool dates, pitted

MAKE YOUR OWN

This is the chapter for those of you who like making recipes from scratch. Here are my plant-based options – all quick, easy and so versatile.

06

OAT MILK

BATCH COOKABLE

FREEZABLE

+5 DAYS

LASTS FOR +5 DAYS IN THE FRIDGE

NUT-FREE

Soak the oats in water for at least 30 minutes or up to overnight, if you like. Drain and rinse, discarding the soaking water. Mix with the fresh measure of water, then strain through a muslin (cheesecloth). Store in the fridge.

MAKES 300 ML (10 FL OZ/1¼ CUPS)

60 g (2 oz/⅔ cup) oats
750 ml (25 fl oz/3 cups) water,
   plus extra to taste

PLANT CREAM

BATCH COOKABLE

FREEZABLE

4-5 DAYS

LASTS FOR 4-5 DAYS IN THE FRIDGE

SUNFLOWER OPTION IS NUT FREE

Here are three versions of quick plant-based creams that can be made super-quickly at home. The almond version lends itself best to sweet recipes.

Regardless of which version you choose, simply put all the ingredients in a blender and blitz until you have the desired smooth texture. If you want an even smoother consistency, put the nuts or seeds and water in the blender jug and leave them to soak for at least 20–30 minutes before blending.

MAKES A 250 ML (8½ FL OZ) JAR

FOR CASHEW CREAM

60 g (2 oz/½ cup) cashews
250 ml (8½ fl oz/1 cup) boiling water

FOR ALMOND CREAM

60 g (2 oz/½ cup) blanched almonds
250 ml (8½ fl oz/1 cup) boiling water

FOR SUNFLOWER CREAM

60 g (2 oz/½ cup) sunflower seeds
250 ml (8½ fl oz/1 cup) boiling water

MAKE YOUR OWN

PLANT MAYO

This is a real treat of a mayonnaise and super-easy to make. It lasts for a good week in the fridge, too. You can save your chickpeas for hummus or any of the other recipes in this book – they last about 3–4 days in the fridge. You can add lots of different flavours to the mayonnaise, such as herbs, spices and more.

Put the aquafaba, lemon juice and apple cider vinegar in a bowl and whisk with an electric whisk until combined. Whisking continuously, gradually begin to add the rapeseed oil until the mixture emulsifies and starts coming together as a mayonnaise. Continue whisking and slowly adding the olive oil until it is all incorporated. Season with mustard, salt and pepper to taste.

**MAKES A 250 ML
(8½ FL OZ/1 CUP) JAR**

3½ tablespoons aquafaba (liquid from tinned chickpeas (garbanzos))
1 tablespoon lemon juice
1 teaspoon apple cider vinegar
120 ml (4 fl oz/½ cup) organic rapeseed oil (organic is usually a lot yellower)
60 ml (2 fl oz/¼ cup) olive oil
1 teaspoon Dijon mustard
1 pinch of salt and freshly cracked black pepper

NUT-FREE PLANT PARMESAN

This is a great alternative to Parmesan cheese. The bouillon adds the saltiness that we so crave. What makes this particularly special is that most plant substitutes for Parmesan are made with nuts so are off limits to anyone with a nut allergy, whereas this can be enjoyed by everyone.

Add all the ingredients to a blender and pulse until you have Parmesan cheese-like consistency. This should be kept in a glass jar in the fridge and lasts for weeks.

MAKES ABOUT 150 G (5 OZ)

125 g (4 oz/1 cup) sunflower seeds
2 tablespoons vegan bouillon (I love the Swiss one)
2 tablespoons nutritional yeast (optional)

BATCH COOKABLE

FREEZABLE

LASTS FOR 3+ DAYS IN THE FRIDGE

NUT-FREE

VEGAN OMELETTE

This is super-versatile and lends itself to lots of different fillings and toppings. This is also a great binder for other recipes, so you'll find it in a few other places in the book, too.

Put all the ingredients except the oil into a bowl and mix well. Heat a medium-sized non-stick frying pan (skillet) over a medium heat and add the olive oil. Pour in the batter and tilt the pan to spread the mixture. Once you see bubbles on the surface, after about 5 minutes, flip it on to the other side and cook for another couple of minutes. Once the omelette is done, either serve hot or place on a plate and let it cool down.

MAKES 1 PORTION

60 g (2 oz/½ cup) chickpea (gram) flour
⅛ teaspoon bicarbonate of soda (baking soda)
1 teaspoon apple cider vinegar
125 ml (4 fl oz/½ cup) water
1 tablespoon olive oil

MENU
PLANNI

Here are three great menu options to
get you going. I have distinguished them
according to the time it will take to prepare
the food, the type of person you might
be and how willing you are to cook from
scratch. In any case, they are fuss-free
and easy to accomplish with a tiny bit
of planning. Let's get going!

THE EASY PEASY WAY: This first menu plan is for the go-getters, the people on the go who just want to get it done as quickly and as painlessly as possible. They are happy to eat the same thing on a regular basis as long as they feel full and satisfied.

FOR THE PLANNERS: This plan is for the people who like to spend a few hours on a Sunday preparing themselves for the week. They like to be organised and don't mind batch cooking a few meals ahead. This plan will give them access to prepared meals a few days in advance and will take away any worries about what to feed themselves next as you will have it all covered.

FAST & FRESH: Here is a plan for those who like to eat fresh and fast, while still putting in the effort to cook from scratch. Quick, simple recipes that take no time to prepare from scratch and can be eaten straight away – that's the aim of the fast-and-fresh eaters. They are happy to put effort in to go beyond just having a sandwich.

THE EASY PEASY WAY

DAY	BREAKFAST	LUNCH	DINNER
MONDAY	Smoothie on the Go (page 16)	Lunch Box Pasta Salad (page 56; make extra for Wednesday)	Butternut, Coconut & Ginger Soup (page 67)
TUESDAY	Smoothie on the Go (page 16)	Herby Quinoa Tabbouleh (page 50; make extra for Thursday)	Five-minute Pea Soup with Onion Bhaji Pancakes (page 62)
WEDNESDAY	Smoothie on the Go (page 16)	Lunch Box Pasta Salad (page 56)	Mexican Nachos Plate (page 64)
THURSDAY	Smoothie on the Go (page 16)	Herby Quinoa Tabbouleh (page 50)	Middle Eastern Traybake (page 98; save one portion for lunch)
FRIDAY	Smoothie on the Go (page 16)	Middle Eastern Traybake (page 98)	Rainbow Curry Rice (page 82)
SATURDAY	Breakfast Burrito (page 26)	Fully Loaded Sweet Potatoes (page 112)	Fridge Raid Soup (page 66)
SUNDAY	Chinese Omelette (page 38)	One-tray Sunday Roast with Smashed Peas (page 116)	Almond Cookies (page 126; sandwiched with ice cream)
SNACK OPTIONS TO TAKE TO WORK	Fifteen-minute Muffins (page 129)	Almond Cookies (page 126)	

THE EASY PEASY SHOPPING LIST

BAKED & BAKING GOODS

- [ ] almond flour
- [ ] baking powder
- [ ] bicarbonate of soda (baking soda)
- [ ] bread
- [ ] brown sugar
- [ ] buckwheat flour
- [ ] chickpea (gram) flour
- [ ] cacao
- [ ] coconut sugar
- [ ] corn chips
- [ ] corn or wheat tortillas
- [ ] dairy-free chocolate, dark or milk
- [ ] flatbreads
- [ ] oat bran
- [ ] rice malt syrup
- [ ] vanilla paste

FRUIT & VEG

- [ ] aubergine (eggplant)
- [ ] avocados
- [ ] baby spinach
- [ ] bananas
- [ ] butternut squash
- [ ] carrots
- [ ] cherry tomatoes
- [ ] chilli
- [ ] Chinese leaves (stem lettuce)
- [ ] courgette (zucchini)
- [ ] frozen blueberries
- [ ] frozen peas
- [ ] garlic cloves
- [ ] ginger root
- [ ] kale
- [ ] leeks
- [ ] lemons
- [ ] limes
- [ ] little gem (bibb) lettuces
- [ ] medjool dates
- [ ] mixed vegetables
- [ ] onions
- [ ] parsnips
- [ ] pineapple
- [ ] pomegranate seeds
- [ ] potato
- [ ] red (bell) peppers
- [ ] red cabbage
- [ ] red onions
- [ ] rocket (arugula) leaves
- [ ] shallots
- [ ] spring onions (scallions)
- [ ] sugar snap peas
- [ ] sweetcorn
- [ ] sweet potatoes
- [ ] tomatoes
- [ ] yellow (bell) pepper

CONDIMENTS, JARS OILS & PICKLES

- [ ] apple cider vinegar
- [ ] chilli jam
- [ ] chilli sauce or sriracha
- [ ] coconut oil
- [ ] flaxseed oil
- [ ] harissa
- [ ] hummus
- [ ] maple syrup
- [ ] olive oil
- [ ] sesame oil
- [ ] sundried tomatoes
- [ ] tahini (sesame paste)
- [ ] tamari
- [ ] vegan stock cubes

HERBS & SPICES

- [ ] allspice
- [ ] barbecue spice mix
- [ ] bay leaves
- [ ] black peppercorns
- [ ] cayenne
- [ ] coriander (cilantro)
- [ ] fajita spice mix
- [ ] freshly cracked black pepper
- [ ] ground cinnamon
- [ ] mint
- [ ] parsley
- [ ] salt
- [ ] sweet paprika
- [ ] turmeric
- [ ] yellow curry powder

PULSES, NUTS & SEEDS

- [ ] black beans
- [ ] butter (lima) beans
- [ ] chickpeas (garbanzos)
- [ ] hazelnuts (filberts) or walnuts
- [ ] hemp hearts
- [ ] peanut butter
- [ ] pumpkin seeds
- [ ] sesame seeds

VEGAN MILKS & CHEESES

- [ ] coconut cream
- [ ] coconut yoghurt
- [ ] GMO-free firm tofu
- [ ] nut butter
- [ ] oat milk
- [ ] plant cream
- [ ] plant mayo
- [ ] plant milk
- [ ] plant yoghurt

PASTA, RICE, NOODLES & GRAINS

- [ ] basmati rice
- [ ] penne pasta
- [ ] quinoa

FOR THE PLANNERS

DAY	BREAKFAST	LUNCH	DINNER
MONDAY	Sweet Quinoa (page 22)	Egg Sandwich (page 48)	Roasted Roots & Peanut Sauce (page 108; save a portion for lunch)
TUESDAY	Sweet Quinoa (page 22)	Roasted Roots & Peanut Sauce (page 108)	Korean Barbecue Roasted Broccoli (page 121)
WEDNESDAY	Spicy Carrot Oats (page 21; make a batch of Spicy Carrot Oats and soak them overnight instead of a porridge)	Ultimate BLT Sandwich (page 49)	Best Burger You Will Ever Eat (page 52; save one for lunch)
THURSDAY	Spicy Carrot Oats (page 21)	Best Burger You Will Ever Eat (page 52)	Veggie Fritters with Sweet Chilli Dip (page 73)
FRIDAY	Fluffy One-pan Pancakes (page 29; make a double batch for Saturday morning)	Herby Quinoa Tabbouleh (page 50)	Creamy Satay Noodles with Salt & Pepper Fried Tofu (page 76)
SATURDAY	Fluffy One-pan Pancakes (page 29)	Five-minute Pea Soup with Onion Bhaji Pancakes (page 62)	Emma's Carrot Mash Shepherd's Pie (page 105; make one and save the other portions for the following week) / Five-minute Fried Banana & Crumble (page 135)
SUNDAY	Avocado Benedict (page 37; save the chickpeas for dinner)	Twenty-minute Green Pasta Bake (page 107; make more and freeze for another day)	Courgettes with Chickpeas (page 110) / 'Chocolate' Salami (page 130)
SNACK OPTIONS TO TAKE TO WORK	Fifteen-minute Muffins (page 129)	Almond Cookies (page 126)	

FOR THE PLANNERS

- ○ Sunday is preparation day.
- ○ Do a shop to make sure you have everything you need for the week.
- ○ Make a batch of Sweet Quinoa (see page 22).
- ○ Make a batch of Hummus (see page 42), save the chickpea water and if you have time make the Plant Mayo (see page 144).
- ○ Make the Bacon for the BLT (see page 49) and store in a glass container in the fridge.
- ○ Make the egg filling for the Egg Sandwich (see page 48).
- ○ Make the patties for the Best Burger (see page 52).

FOR THE PLANNERS SHOPPING LIST

BAKED & BAKING GOODS

- [ ] almond flour
- [ ] baking powder
- [ ] bicarbonate of soda (baking soda)
- [ ] brown sugar
- [ ] buckwheat flour
- [ ] burger buns
- [ ] cacao
- [ ] cacao nibs
- [ ] chickpea (gram) flour
- [ ] coconut sugar
- [ ] currants
- [ ] raisins
- [ ] oat bran
- [ ] oat flour
- [ ] oats
- [ ] rice malt syrup
- [ ] sourdough
- [ ] vanilla paste
- [ ] vegan cookies

CONDIMENTS, JARS, OILS & PICKLES

- [ ] apple cider vinegar
- [ ] capers (baby capers)
- [ ] chilli jam
- [ ] coconut oil
- [ ] cornichons
- [ ] Dijon mustard
- [ ] harissa
- [ ] hummus
- [ ] jam
- [ ] maple syrup
- [ ] olive oil
- [ ] organic rapeseed oil
- [ ] passata (sieved tomatoes)
- [ ] sesame oil
- [ ] tomato ketchup
- [ ] tahini (sesame paste)
- [ ] tamari
- [ ] vegan stock cubes

FRUIT & VEG

- [ ] avocado
- [ ] baby spinach
- [ ] bananas
- [ ] blood oranges or oranges
- [ ] broccoli
- [ ] carrots
- [ ] cavolo nero
- [ ] celeriac
- [ ] chestnut mushrooms
- [ ] chilli
- [ ] courgette (zucchini)
- [ ] eating (dessert) apples
- [ ] frozen peas
- [ ] garlic cloves
- [ ] ginger root
- [ ] green (bell) peppers
- [ ] green salad
- [ ] greens
- [ ] kale
- [ ] leeks
- [ ] lemons
- [ ] little gem (bibb) lettuce
- [ ] medjool dates
- [ ] mushrooms
- [ ] onions
- [ ] parsnip
- [ ] pineapple
- [ ] pears
- [ ] potatoes
- [ ] rainbow chard
- [ ] red (bell) peppers
- [ ] red onions
- [ ] seasonal fruits
- [ ] shallots
- [ ] spring onions (scallions)
- [ ] tomatoes
- [ ] watercress
- [ ] yellow (bell) peppers

HERBS & SPICES

- [ ] allspice
- [ ] barbecue spice mix
- [ ] bay leaf
- [ ] cayenne
- [ ] chives
- [ ] coriander (cilantro)
- [ ] dill
- [ ] fenugreek seeds
- [ ] freshly cracked black pepper
- [ ] ground cardamom
- [ ] ground cinnamon
- [ ] ground cloves
- [ ] herbes de Provence
- [ ] Jamaican jerk spice
- [ ] mint
- [ ] parsley
- [ ] salt
- [ ] sweet paprika
- [ ] tarragon
- [ ] thyme
- [ ] turmeric
- [ ] yellow curry powder

PASTA, RICE, NOODLES & GRAINS

- [ ] brown rice
- [ ] long-grain basmati rice
- [ ] penne pasta
- [ ] quinoa
- [ ] rice noodles

PULSES, NUTS & SEEDS

- [ ] black beans
- [ ] chickpeas (garbanzos)
- [ ] chopped almonds
- [ ] chopped nuts
- [ ] flaxseed meal
- [ ] hazelnuts (filberts) or walnuts
- [ ] hemp hearts
- [ ] nut butter
- [ ] peanut butter
- [ ] red lentils
- [ ] sesame seeds
- [ ] unsalted roasted peanuts
- [ ] walnuts

VEGAN MILKS & CHEESES

- [ ] coconut yoghurt
- [ ] GMO-free extra-firm tofu
- [ ] GMO-free smoked tofu
- [ ] nut butter
- [ ] oat milk
- [ ] plant cream
- [ ] plant mayo
- [ ] plant yoghurt

FAST & FRESH

DAY	BREAKFAST	LUNCH	DINNER
MONDAY	Tender Greens on Toast with Pea Hummus (page 32)	Tokyo Hummus Sandwich (page 42; make two and save one for lunch the next day)	Faux Tuna Melt Toastie (page 44)
TUESDAY	Banoffee Oats (page 20)	Tokyo Hummus Sandwich (page 42)	Quick Laksa (page 60)
WEDNESDAY	Tender Greens on Toast with Ajvar (page 32)	Leafy Green Fried Rice (page 94)	Zanzibar Potatoes & Spinach (page 81)
THURSDAY	Mostly Apple & Oat Porridge (page 19)	Mexican Nacho Plate (page 64)	Pasta e Fagioli (page 89)
FRIDAY	Savoury Ginger & Garlic Oats (page 31)	My Ethiopian Rice (page 88; this can be saved as an extra portion too)	Pytt i Panna (page 95) / Griddled Pineapple & Chilli Flakes (page 125)
SATURDAY	Breakfast Burrito (page 26)	Japanese Soba Noodle Soup (page 59)	Carbonara (page 134) / Two-minute Ice Cream (page 134)
SUNDAY	Chinese Omelette (page 38)	Herb-crusted Portobello & Creamed Spinach (page 118)	Cauliflower Steaks (page 102) / Peanut Butter Chocolate Pots (page 135)
SNACK OPTIONS TO TAKE TO WORK	Fifteen-minute Muffins (page 129)	Almond Cookies (page 126)	

FAST & FRESH

- ○ Prepare by buying all the ingredients.
- ○ Everything will be made from scratch with similar ingredients.
- ○ Quick, fresh, fuss-free and delicious.

FAST & FRESH SHOPPING LIST

BAKED & BAKING GOODS

- [ ] almond flour
- [ ] baking powder
- [ ] bicarbonate of soda (baking soda)
- [ ] bread
- [ ] brown or coconut sugar
- [ ] cacao
- [ ] chickpea (gram) flour
- [ ] corn chips
- [ ] corn or wheat tortillas
- [ ] dark dairy-free chocolate (with at least 70% cocoa solids)
- [ ] dark dairy-free chocolate chips
- [ ] oats
- [ ] sourdough
- [ ] vanilla paste

PASTA, RICE, NOODLES & GRAINS

- [ ] long-grain basmati rice
- [ ] penne pasta
- [ ] rice noodles
- [ ] soba noodles
- [ ] spaghetti
- [ ] sushi rice

PULSES, NUTS & SEEDS

- [ ] black beans
- [ ] black sesame seeds
- [ ] blanched almonds
- [ ] borlotti beans
- [ ] brown beans
- [ ] cashews
- [ ] chickpeas (garbanzos)
- [ ] chopped nuts
- [ ] hemp hearts
- [ ] nut butter
- [ ] peanut butter
- [ ] sesame seeds
- [ ] toasted nuts
- [ ] walnuts

FRUIT & VEG

- [ ] aubergine (eggplant)
- [ ] avocados
- [ ] bananas
- [ ] beetroot (beet) slices
- [ ] berries
- [ ] carrots
- [ ] cauliflower
- [ ] cherry tomatoes
- [ ] chillies
- [ ] Chinese leaves (stem lettuce)
- [ ] eating (dessert) apples
- [ ] fresh or tinned pineapple
- [ ] frozen peas
- [ ] garlic cloves
- [ ] ginger root
- [ ] kale
- [ ] leeks
- [ ] lemons
- [ ] lettuce
- [ ] limes
- [ ] medjool dates
- [ ] mushrooms
- [ ] onions
- [ ] pak choy (bok choy)
- [ ] pineapple
- [ ] pomegranate seeds
- [ ] portobello mushrooms
- [ ] potatoes
- [ ] red onions
- [ ] shallots
- [ ] spinach leaves
- [ ] spring onions (scallions)
- [ ] swede
- [ ] sweet potatoes
- [ ] tenderstem broccoli
- [ ] tinned artichokes
- [ ] tomatoes
- [ ] yellow (bell) pepper

CONDIMENTS, JARS, OILS & PICKLES

- [ ] apple cider vinegar
- [ ] chilli jam
- [ ] chilli sauce
- [ ] coconut oil
- [ ] cornichons
- [ ] Dijon mustard
- [ ] grilled jarred red peppers
- [ ] jam
- [ ] maple syrup
- [ ] miso paste
- [ ] nori sheets
- [ ] olive oil
- [ ] pickled ginger
- [ ] rice malt syrup
- [ ] sesame oil
- [ ] sriracha
- [ ] tahini (sesame paste)
- [ ] tamari
- [ ] tomato purée (paste)
- [ ] vegan stock cubes

HERBS & SPICES

- [ ] allspice
- [ ] basil leaves
- [ ] cardamom pods
- [ ] cayenne
- [ ] chilli (hot pepper) flakes
- [ ] chilli powder
- [ ] coriander (cilantro)
- [ ] coriander seeds
- [ ] cumin seeds
- [ ] dill
- [ ] fajita spice mix
- [ ] fenugreek seeds
- [ ] freshly cracked black pepper
- [ ] ground cardamom
- [ ] ground cinnamon
- [ ] ground cloves
- [ ] ground cumin
- [ ] mint
- [ ] parsley
- [ ] rosemary
- [ ] salt
- [ ] sweet paprika
- [ ] thyme
- [ ] turmeric

VEGAN MILKS & CHEESES

- [ ] coconut cream
- [ ] coconut milk
- [ ] coconut yoghurt
- [ ] oat milk
- [ ] plant cheese
- [ ] plant cream
- [ ] plant mayo
- [ ] plant Parmesan
- [ ] plant yoghurt

ACKNOWLEDGEMENTS

I'd like to thank my family for all the support that I have received over the years in continuing to follow my passion – including my own little family that comes with me on all of these adventures.

To Hardie Grant, especially Kate, for enabling me to be so creatively involved in the book process.

To Sam and Sara for being there from the early days, and always helping out with invaluable advice and kindness.

To Sara and Niki for being my rocks, foodie friends and all-round amazing women.

Thank you also to Derek, Chantelle and Gennaro for their kind words; it means a bunch coming from such legends.

To Jamie Oliver for being an early supporter, and a caring human being. Your kindness and big heart inspire us all to be better.

There are so many people along the way that have made things possible; it's like those drawings with numbers that connect all the dots. In my case, there are hundreds of connectors that have led me to where I am today. You all know who you are. Thank you with all my heart.

ABOUT BETTINA

Bettina Campolucci Bordi is a freelance chef and food blogger at Bettina's Kitchen. Specialising in vegan and gluten-free cuisine, cooking has been a constant in Bettina's life, from her experiences of her childhood spent in Denmark, Tanzania and Sweden, following her through to her teens and into adulthood, before studying at the Matthew Kenney Culinary Academy in Los Angeles. She's run workshops and cookery classes, advised clients on food intolerances and allergies, consulted on recipes, launched pop-ups, hosted wellness retreats around the world, and built a large, loyal Instagram following. This is her second book; her first, *Happy Food*, was published in 2018.

bettinaskitchen.com
@bettinas_kitchen

INDEX

Published in 2019 by Hardie Grant Books,
an imprint of Hardie Grant Publishing

Hardie Grant Books (London)
5th & 6th Floors
52–54 Southwark Street
London SE1 1UN

Hardie Grant Books (Melbourne)
Building 1, 658 Church Street
Richmond, Victoria 3121

hardiegrantbooks.com

British Library Cataloguing-in-Publication Data.
A catalogue record for this book is available from the British Library.

7 Day Vegan Challenge
ISBN: 978-1-78488-283-9

10 9 8 7 6 5 4 3 2

Publishing Director: Kate Pollard
Senior Editor: Eve Marleau
Design: Evi-O. Studio | Susan Le
Typesetting: Evi-O. Studio | Rosie Whelan & Nicole Ho
Photographer: Nassima Rothacker
Food Stylist: Bettina Campolucci Bordi
Prop Stylist: Tamzin Ferdinando
Editor: Wendy Hobson
Proofreader: Kay Delves
Indexer: Vanessa Bird

Colour reproduction by p2d
Printed and bound in China by Leo Paper Products Ltd.

MIX
Paper from
responsible sources
FSC® C020056
FSC
www.fsc.org